Regional Development through Ecological Business

Regional disparity is one of the most pressing social issues current today. Many countries lack the basic infrastructure to establishing new businesses or industrial clusters. This book argues that existing economic theories which have tended to focus on macroscopic views of society or industries may be misguided. It delivers a refreshing insight from a microscopic viewpoint of enterprise/business management and shows how businesses can achieve sustainable development at the level of enterprise.

The book includes case studies to illustrate how a successful model can be put in place to effect sustainable development at enterprise level. The implementation of sustainable development is also closely connected to knowledge management. This knowledge management involves intangible assets such as tacit knowledge, social capital, ecological resources, art and so forth. It is also closely related to regional issues. This book bridges the relationship between knowledge management and regional issues from the standpoint of sustainable development and illustrates how they can be integrated to overcome the constraints to grow.

The well-founded and clearly presented research of this book makes it a useful reference for students, researchers and businesses.

Makoto Hirano received an MBA degree from Temple University in the US and a PhD in International Business from Waseda University in Japan. For the past seven years he has been involved in research around regional development issues. He has visited more than two hundred enterprises and organizations in different regions of the world in order to study new management models for contemporary business related to the design of sustainable regional communities and the creation of intangible assets through art.

Routledge studies in the modern world economy

1 **Interest Rates and Budget Deficits**
A study of the advanced economies
Kanhaya L Gupta and Bakhtiar Moazzami

2 **World Trade after the Uruguay Round**
Prospects and policy options for the twenty-first century
Edited by Harald Sander and András Inotai

3 **The Flow Analysis of Labour Markets**
Edited by Ronald Schettkat

4 **Inflation and Unemployment**
Contributions to a new macroeconomic approach
Edited by Alvaro Cencini and Mauro Baranzini

5 **Macroeconomic Dimensions of Public Finance**
Essays in honour of Vito Tanzi
Edited by Mario I. Blejer and Teresa M. Ter-Minassian

6 **Fiscal Policy and Economic Reforms**
Essays in honour of Vito Tanzi
Edited by Mario I. Blejer and Teresa M. Ter-Minassian

7 **Competition Policy in the Global Economy**
Modalities for co-operation
Edited by Leonard Waverman, William S. Comanor and Akira Goto

8 **Working in the Macro Economy**
A study of the US labor market
Martin F. J. Prachowny

9 **How Does Privatization Work?**
Edited by Anthony Bennett

10 **The Economics and Politics of International Trade**
Freedom and trade: volume II
Edited by Gary Cook

11 **The Legal and Moral Aspects of International Trade**
Freedom and trade: volume III
Edited by Asif Qureshi, Hillel Steiner and Geraint Parry

12 **Capital Markets and Corporate Governance in Japan, Germany and the United States**
Organizational response to market inefficiencies
Helmut M. Dietl

13 **Competition and Trade Policies**
Coherence or conflict
Edited by Einar Hope

14 **Rice**
The primary commodity
A. J. H. Latham

15 **Trade, Theory and Econometrics**
Essays in honour of John S. Chipman
Edited by James C. Moore, Raymond Riezman and James R. Melvin

16 **Who benefits from Privatisation?**
Edited by Moazzem Hossain and Justin Malbon

17 **Towards a Fair Global Labour Market**
Avoiding the new slave trade
Ozay Mehmet, Errol Mendes and Robert Sinding

18 **Models of Futures Markets**
Edited by Barry Goss

19 **Venture Capital Investment**
An agency analysis of UK practice
Gavin C. Reid

20 **Macroeconomic Forecasting**
A sociological appraisal
Robert Evans

21 **Multimedia and Regional Economic Restructuring**
Edited by Hans-Joachim Braczyk, Gerhard Fuchs and Hans-Georg Wolf

22 **The New Industrial Geography**
Regions, regulation and institutions
Edited by Trevor J. Barnes and Meric S. Gertler

23 **The Employment Impact of Innovation**
Evidence and policy
Edited by Marco Vivarelli and Mario Pianta

24 **International Health Care Reform**
A legal, economic and political analysis
Colleen Flood

25 **Competition Policy Analysis**
Edited by Einar Hope

26 **Culture and Enterprise**
The development, representation and morality of business
Don Lavoie and Emily Chamlee-Wright

27 **Global Financial Crises and Reforms**
Cases and caveats
B. N. Ghosh

28 **Geography of Production and Economic Integration**
Miroslav N. Jovanović

29 **Technology, Trade and Growth in OECD Countries**
Does specialisation matter?
Valentina Meliciani

30 **Post-Industrial Labour Markets**
Profiles of North America and Scandinavia
Edited by Thomas P. Boje and Bengt Furaker

31 **Capital Flows without Crisis**
Reconciling capital mobility and economic stability
Edited by Dipak Dasgupta, Marc Uzan and Dominic Wilson

32 **International Trade and National Welfare**
Murray C. Kemp

33 **Global Trading Systems at Crossroads**
A post-Seattle perspective
Dilip K. Das

34 **The Economics and Management of Technological Diversification**
Edited by John Cantwell, Alfonso Gambardella and Ove Granstrand

35 **Before and Beyond EMU**
Historical lessons and future prospects
Edited by Patrick Crowley

36 **Fiscal Decentralization**
Ehtisham Ahmad and Vito Tanzi

37 **Regionalisation of Globalised Innovation**
Locations for advanced industrial development and disparities in participation
Edited by Ulrich Hilpert

38 **Gold and the Modern World Economy**
Edited by MoonJoong Tcha

39 **Global Economic Institutions**
Willem Molle

40 **Global Governance and Financial Crises**
Edited by Meghnad Desai and Yahia Said

41 **Linking Local and Global Economies**
The ties that bind
Edited by Carlo Pietrobelli and Arni Sverrisson

42 **Tax Systems and Tax Reforms in Europe**
Edited by Luigi Bernardi and Paola Profeta

43 **Trade Liberalization and APEC**
Edited by Jiro Okamoto

44 **Fiscal Deficits in the Pacific Region**
Edited by Akira Kohsaka

45 **Financial Globalization and the Emerging Market Economies**
Dilip K. Das

46 **International Labor Mobility**
Unemployment and increasing returns to scale
Bharati Basu

47 **Good Governance in the Era of Global Neoliberalism**
Conflict and depolitization in Latin America, Eastern Europe, Asia and Africa
Edited by Jolle Demmers, Alex E. Fernández Jilberto and Barbara Hogenboom

48 **The International Trade System**
Alice Landau

49 **International Perspectives on Temporary Work and Workers**
Edited by John Burgess and Julia Connell

50 **Working Time and Workers' Preferences in Industrialized Countries**
Finding the balance
Edited by Jon C. Messenger

51 **Tax Systems and Tax Reforms in New EU Members**
Edited by Luigi Bernardi, Mark Chandler and Luca Gandullia

52 **Globalization and the Nation State**
The impact of the IMF and the World Bank
Edited by Gustav Ranis, James Vreeland and Stephen Kosak

53 **Macroeconomic Policies and Poverty Reduction**
Edited by Ashoka Mody and Catherine Pattillo

54 **Regional Monetary Policy**
Carlos J. Rodríguez-Fuentez

55 **Trade and Migration in the Modern World**
Carl Mosk

56 **Globalisation and the Labour Market**
Trade, technology and less-skilled workers in Europe and the United States
Edited by Robert Anderton, Paul Brenton and John Whalley

57 **Financial Crises**
Socio-economic causes and institutional context
Brenda Spotton Visano

58 Globalization and Self Determination
Is the nation-state under siege?
Edited by David R. Cameron, Gustav Ranis and Annalisa Zinn

59 Developing Countries and the Doha Development Round of the WTO
Edited by Pitou van Dijck and Gerrit Faber

60 Immigrant Enterprise in Europe and the USA
Prodromos Panayiotopoulos

61 Solving the Riddle of Globalization and Development
Edited by Manuel Agosín, David Bloom, George Chapelier and Jagdish Saigal

62 Foreign Direct Investment and the World Economy
Ashoka Mody

63 The World Economy
A global analysis
Horst Siebert

64 Production Organizations in Japanese Economic Development
Edited by Tetsuji Okazaki

65 The Economics of Language
International analyses
Edited by Barry R. Chiswick and Paul W. Miller

66 Street Entrepreneurs
People, place and politics in local and global perspective
Edited by John Cross and Alfonso Morales

67 Global Challenges and Local Responses
The East Asian experience
Edited by Jang-Sup Shin

68 Globalization and Regional Integration
The origins, development and impact of the single European aviation market
Alan Dobson

69 Russia Moves into the Global Economy
Breaking out
John M. Letiche

70 The European Economy in an American Mirror
Barry Eichengreen, Michael Landesmann and Dieter Stiefel

71 Working Time Around the World
Trends in working hours, laws, and policies in a global comparative perspective
Jon C. Messenger, Sangheon Lee and Deidre McCann

72 International Water Treaties
Negotiation and cooperation along transboundary rivers
Shlomi Dinar

73 Economic Integration in the Americas
Edited by Joseph A. McKinney and H. Stephen Gardner

74 Expanding Frontiers of Global Trade Rules
The political economy dynamics of the international trading system
Nitya Nanda

75 The Macroeconomics of Global Imbalances
European and Asian perspectives
Edited by Marc Uzan

76 China and Asia
Economic and financial interactions
Edited by Yin-Wong Cheung and Kar-Yiu Wong

77 **Regional Inequality in China**
Trends, explanations and policy responses
Edited by Shenggen Fan, Ravi Kanbur and Xiaobo Zhang

78 **Governing Rapid Growth in China**
Equity and institutions
Edited by Ravi Kanbur and Xiaobo Zhang

79 **The Indonesian Labour Market**
Shafiq Dhanani, Iyanatul Islam and Anis Chowdhury

80 **Cost-Benefit Analysis in Multi-level Government in Europe and the USA**
The case of EU cohesion policy and US federal investment policies
Alessandro Ferrara

81 **The Economic Geography of Air Transportation**
Space, time, and the freedom of the sky
John Bowen

82 **Cartelization, Antitrust and Globalization in the US and Europe**
Mark LeClair

83 **The Political Economy of Integration**
Jeffrey Cason

84 **Critical Issues in Air Transport Economics and Business**
Rosario Macario and Eddy Van de Voorde

85 **Financial Liberalisation and Economic Performance**
Luiz Fernando de Paula

86 **A General Theory of Institutional Change**
Shiping Tang

87 **The Dynamics of Asian Financial Integration**
Edited by Michael Devereux, Philip Lane, Park Cyn-young and Wei Shang-jin

88 **Innovative Fiscal Policy and Economic Development in Transition Economies**
Aleksandr Gevorkyan

89 **Foreign Direct Investments in Asia**
Edited by Chalongphob Sussangkarn, Yung Chul Park and Sung Jin Kang

90 **Time Zones, Communications Networks, and International Trade**
Toru Kikuchi

91 **Miraculous Growth and Stagnation in Post-War Japan**
Edited by Koichi Hamada, Keijiro Otsuka, Gustav Ranis, and Ken Togo

92 **Multilateralism and Regionalism in Global Economic Governance**
Trade, investment and finance
Edited by Junji Nakagawa

93 **Economic Growth and Income Inequality in China, India and Singapore**
Trends and policy implications
Pundarik Mukhopadhaya, G. Shantakumar and Bhanoji Rao

94 **Foreign Direct Investment in China**
Spillover effects on domestic enterprises
Deng Ziliang

95 **Enterprise Forms and Economic Efficiency**
Capitalist, cooperative and government firms
Kazuhiko Mikami

96 Diversity and Transformations of Asian Capitalism
Edited by R. Boyer, H. Uemura and A. Isogai

97 Knowledge Transfer in the Automobile Industry
Global-local production networks
Dessy Irawati

98 Exchange Rates and Foreign Direct Investment in Emerging Asia
Selected issues and policy options
Ramkishen S. Rajan

99 Singapore, the Energy Economy
From the first refinery to the end of cheap oil, 1960–2010
Ng Weng Hoong

100 China-India Economics
Challenges, competition and collaboration
Amitendu Palit

101 Case Studies on Chinese Enterprises
Edited by Donglin Xia

102 Argentina's Economic Growth and Recovery
Michael Cohen

103 The Korean Labour Market After the 1997 Economic Crisis
Edited by Joonmo Cho, Richard B. Freeman, Jaeho Keum and Sunwoong Kim

104 China and India
The quest for energy resources in the 21st century
Zhao Hong

105 Beyond the Global Crisis
Structural adjustments and regional integration in Europe and Latin America
Edited by Lionello Punzo, Carmen Aparecida Feio and Martin Putchet Anyui

106 The Global Economic Crisis in Latin America
Impacts and responses
Edited by Michael Cohen

107 The Processes and Practices of Fair Trade
Trust, ethics and governance
Edited by Brigitte Granville and Janet Dine

108 Regional Development through Ecological Business
Unique cases in Japanese rural regions
Makoto Hirano

Regional Development through Ecological Business

Unique cases in Japanese rural regions

Makoto Hirano

Routledge
Taylor & Francis Group
LONDON AND NEW YORK

First published 2013
by Routledge
2 Park Square, Milton Park, Abingdon, Oxon OX14 4RN

Simultaneously published in the USA and Canada
by Routledge
711 Third Avenue, New York, NY 10017

Routledge is an imprint of the Taylor & Francis Group, an informa business

First issued in paperback 2014

British Library Cataloguing in Publication Data
A catalogue record for this book is available from the British Library

Library of Congress Cataloging in Publication Data
Regional development through ecological business : unique cases in Japanese rural regions / [edited by] Makoto Hirano.
p. cm. – (Routledge studies in the modern world economy ; 109)
Includes bibliographical references and index.
1. Regional planning–Japan. 2. Rural development–Japan.
3. Sustainable development–Japan. I. Hirano, Makoto.
HT395.J3R434 2012
307.1'4120952–dc23 2012008700

ISBN: 978-0-415-69441-4 (hbk)
ISBN: 978-0-415-70523-3 (pbk)

Typeset in Times New Roman
by Wearset Ltd, Boldon, Tyne and Wear

Contents

Illustrations

Figures

Table

Preface

Regional disparity is one of the most pressing current social issues in many countries.

Many economists have argued for regional development from the macroscopic viewpoint of public policy, such as industrial clustering. However, ideas from the microscopic viewpoint of individual businesses/enterprises are also strongly needed for regional development. Furthermore, the mental development of regional people and support for their autonomy are key issues in resource-poor rural areas.

Over seven years I have visited more than 200 enterprises in rural parts of Japan, China, Spain, the UK, and Germany in order to obtain some clues to solving the issue of regional disparity. I interviewed numerous business people about their management strategies and behaviors. Through these interviews I found that many enterprises in rural regions of Japan showed interesting similarities regarding their approach to organization management and developing business resources. Some of these businesses might be called "ecological style of businesses," and others might be called "businesses based on intangible assets."

Gradually, I came to recognize that these enterprises represent a new wave of business innovation, not only for the regional people involved but also for all contemporary people endeavouring to survive in a recently globalized world facing "The Limits to Growth." My current research work is dominated by the concept of "sustainable development," that is, development that does not destroy the nature of the Earth. This is now a universal issue for many people and many enterprises.

In March 2011, Japan experienced a terrible disaster which critically affected nuclear plants. Many people – not only the Japanese but also many other nationalities – recognized that an ecological style of business for sustainable development is becoming more and more important in the current world.

This book, focusing on unique case histories in Japanese rural regions, is my initial contribution to this research theme. I hope it can contribute in some part to solving the problem of "The Limits to Growth."

February 2012
Makoto Hirano

1 Introduction

Regional development is not merely an issue for regional people. Solving the problem of regional disparity and establishing prosperity in the regions is beneficial even for urban people because it will contribute to an increase in the national product and hence national prosperity. However, regional development is important for everyone not only at this macroscopic economic level but also at the microscopic level of the individual enterprise/business.

One aspect of this is the issue of how to create and establish new businesses without using a lot of resources. Because many resource-poor rural regions lack business resources such as advanced technologies, large factories, natural resources (such as oil or minerals), or large budgets for developing industries, they need to create and establish businesses that do not require many resources. Ways of creating and establishing new businesses with few resources is now highly relevant for everyone.

These ways directly address how we are to overcome the profound problems around the destruction of the Earth's environment, deficiencies of food and/or water, scarce energy, the population explosion, and so on. Because these issues are caused or at least exacerbated by modern industries and mass production, an understanding of business or economic development without resource consumption will help us all.

Ever since the industrial revolution of the eighteenth century, mass production in manufacturing has been responsible for huge and radical growth in both industries and the economy. There was a general belief that this growth was a desirable thing for human beings and society because it brought individual wealth, economic prosperity and better lives. Also, even in the age of mass consumption and surplus supply in the twentieth century, business people believed in the importance of major innovation to enhance competitiveness and create new demand in fresh markets. In those centuries, innovation was mainly thought of as part of the conventional thinking that only large and drastic growth of industries and the economy can bring us happiness.

Even now, concerning investment in start-up enterprises, venture capitalists always invest their money with a view to getting high returns from successful start-ups, because venture business is highly risky and the possibility of success is very small. Consequently these start-ups, invested in by such capitalists, have a similar desire to get high returns by penetrating large markets with major innovation and huge business drive. In that sense, they are aiming in principle for what we call J-curve growth. An aggressive fighting approach producing strong business and "the survival of the fittest" is fundamental to the thinking behind markets and industry across the capitalism world.

However, since the late twentieth century, the situation of industries globally has been changing. Many people began to recognize that large-scale industrial and economic growth caused drastic destruction of natural and residential environments, as well as the depletion of natural resources across many fields, including energy (oil, gas, etc.), food (agricultural products, fish, etc.) and minerals. In addition, speculative economic activity was seen to have a bubble-like character – first growing dramatically and then suddenly and damagingly collapsing. Through experience of the 'bubble' economy, many people began to understand that it is dangerous to pursue drastic economical growth with its money-oriented strategy without also considering the other factors that bring us happiness and peace.

On the business management side, people came to recognize the significance of intangible assets like brand value, tacit knowledge as a seed of innovation, employee satisfaction, motivation, morale and loyalty, enterprise culture, social credibility and responsibility, human relationships, human networks, and so on. These intangible assets became thought of as new resources for business creation or even business itself. Such thinking raised the question of whether there should be a new measure to evaluate industry, the economy, and even innovation. And a new principle for the development of both industry and society.

Innovation is a device for business creation, introducing a new idea, a new resource and a tool for establishing a better market environment surrounding the enterprise. In the past, the two aspects – how dramatically to change conventional markets and how dramatically to create a new market – were thought to be key for evaluating innovation. However, globalization in the late twentieth century made the world comparatively smaller and it is consequently more difficult to maintain the Earth's natural environment by conventional means. In this age, the two questions, how to maintain and not destroy the ecology and natural balances of the Earth and how to sustainably and stably advance markets and society, have became key in discussions of human survival. In this context, the quantity of intangible assets and happiness produced for people by an innovation might be the crucial factor in its evaluation, rather than how much money it earned. How to characterize such sustainable-type – or ecological-type – business innovations and how to create them are our most urgent issues.

In this book, I focus on these new types of business innovation, in search of clues to our survival in the new era. On March 11, 2011, Japanese people experienced a terrible disaster which impacted on nuclear plants. The significance of ecological business is now much more recognized than before. We can learn how to create it by observing many existing cases in rural regions. These cases also show us how to create happiness through business. They demonstrate the establishment of business in a new and contemporary manner, as well as many instances of regional development.

The readers of this book will be exposed to many interesting individual case histories from Japanese rural regions. Some of them are highly entertaining, funny and surprising. For example, the account of the business of selling leaves and the story of the Seashore Museum reveal unique business projects for the development of regional people. If it is possible to sell leaves in mountains and build a museum on a seashore without large sums of money, it should be possible to establish other businesses without capital investment. Please think about this as you read the book.

2 Literature review

The Limits to Growth and regional development

2.1 The impact of *The Limits to Growth*

In this chapter we will look back to the issue raised by the famous book, titled "The Limits to Growth," which was the first trigger of arguments over how to realize sustainable development.

It is popularly understood that the first prediction of the limits to economic growth of current society was expressed in 1972 by the Club of Rome, which consisted of the MIT research group, D. H. Meadows and colleagues.

They published *The Limits to Growth: A Report for The Club of Rome's Project on the Predicament of Mankind* (Meadows *et al.* 1972). It pointed out that world population, industrialization, pollution, food production, and utilization of natural resources would face limits to growth within a hundred years, if they continued to grow at their existing rate. This prediction has already come true in areas such as energy consumption, mineral resources, food production, environmental pollution, climate change resulting from carbon dioxide levels, and so forth.

They pointed out that many changes of the principle parameters for the survival of mankind are expressed as multiple functions. One good example is population. Strictly, population can be determined as a function of birth rate and death rate, as shown in Figure 2.1. Birth rate operates positively and death rate operates negatively on total population, but in many cases the former affects more dominantly and as a result the total population has a tendency to multiply increase, as shown in Figure 2.2.

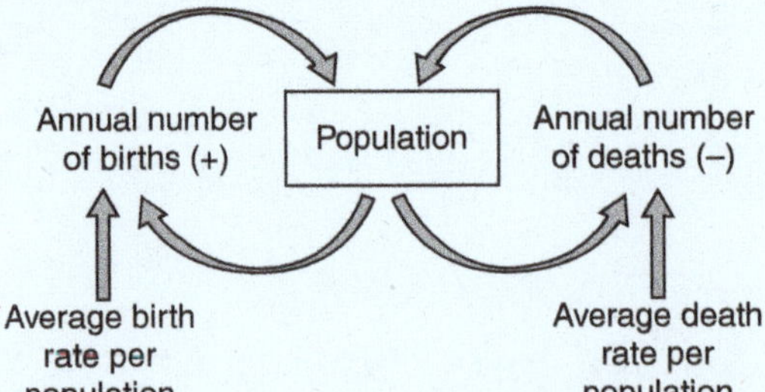

Figure 2.1 Function of population change (source: Meadows *et al.* 1972).

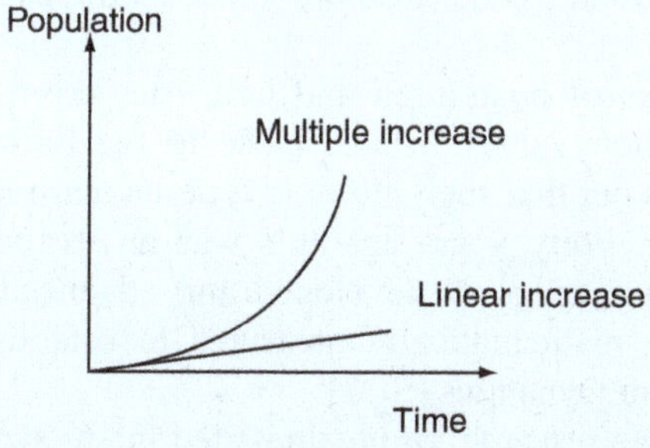

Figure 2.2 Multiple increase of population.

Analogically, many other phenomena can be understood in their multiple-increase tendency in terms of their functionality.

Another straightforward example involves the calculation of interest. Compound interest operates on a principle of multiple-increase so that debt from bank increases multiply. If someone invests money in a business by borrowing from a bank, it is obvious that he/she needs to earn more money than multiply increasing debt by advancing the business. One means to create adequate business profit is to scale up production and thus in many cases business people aim for mass production for the largest possible market.

Of course, in the era of zero-interest or very low interest, the increase of compound interest will be small. However, if it is not a debt but an investment by capitalists, eventually the invested enterprises will be expected to grow according to the J-curve model in order to produce a sufficient return for the whole investment of capital. Investors need to make up the deficit due to the risks of investment by higher rates of return from their successful business projects. In that sense, the numbers of the ratios, such as ROA, ROE and ROI, are extremely important indicators for investors and top managers.

So, most industries will have a tendency to operate by producing multiple-type growth as shown in Figure 2.3, and people are generally more conscious of

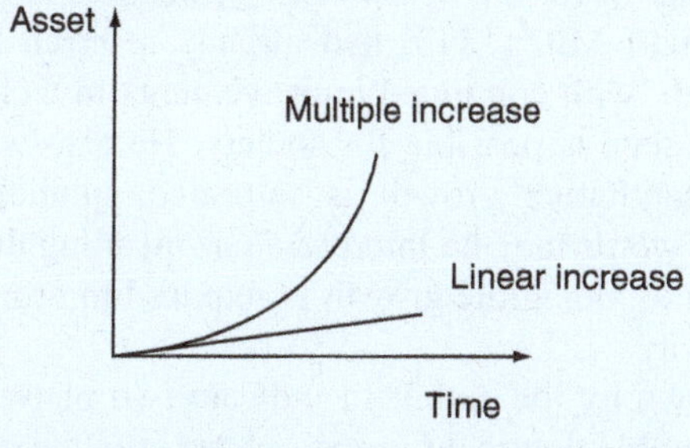

Figure 2.3 Multiple growth of assets.

the rate of increase of sales/revenue than of the absolute value of increase in comparison with past values.

If those multiple growth tendencies of population and industries are maintained for a long time, in the end their values will be close to the limits to growth. *The Limits to Growth* pointed out that such multiple-type increase leads inevitably to a catastrophic situation. Forty years ago this was an extremely important predictive report for human beings. It developed and advanced the methodology of prediction by using mathematically measures to establish a valuable simulation tool called "System Dynamics (SD)."

Having a good command of SD, the research group simulated many aspects of population growth and other environmental problems.

The report was translated into around 29 languages and over nine million copies were published all over the world. The results of the simulation and their implications have impacted on numerous economists, politicians, activists and top managers, stimulating them to pursue ways to avoid the crisis and solve the predicament issues of economic development.

In the conference of the United Nations (World Commission for Environment and Development, WCED) in 1987, the report titled "Our Common Future" presented the concept of "sustainable development." It outlined a harmonized way of maintaining the Earth's ecological environment alongside its economic development.

Subsequently, many economists and sociologists developed concepts related to sustainable development. Brown (2001) proposed an "Eco-Economy" to protect ecological circumstances from drastic development by conventional industries; Gray (1998) pointed out "The Delusion of Global Capitalism" in order to engender respect for locality and the diversity of regions and protect them from American globalism; Hawken *et al.* (1999) proposed "Natural Capitalism" for the protection of the Earth's natural resources; and Korten (1998) outlined his ideas for "The Post-Corporate World", with a return to human-scale enterprise through a change from shareholder ownership to stakeholder ownership. Over a couple of decades, economists and sociologists alike discussed how to modify the conventional economic system to harmonize with the Earth's ecological system, using keywords like ecology, natural resource, localization, regional community, human scale, and so forth.

Daly (1996) mentioned, in his book *Beyond Growth: The Economics of Sustainable Development*, that John Stuart Mill (1848) had already referred to a "stationary state" of economic growth, with continued improvements in technology and ethics, arguing that such a state is possible for society. He also wrote that, if economic, materialistic, quantitative growth is saturated, qualitative development should be pursued. His words may be interpreted as meaning that a shift from tangible economic growth to intangible growth is required in order to avoid the predicament of future scarcity.

Figure 2.4 was schematically drawn by the author to indicate two phases of the growth of an asset; one is the tangible dominant growth phase, and the other is the intangible dominant growth phase. Most of the stages of mass-production

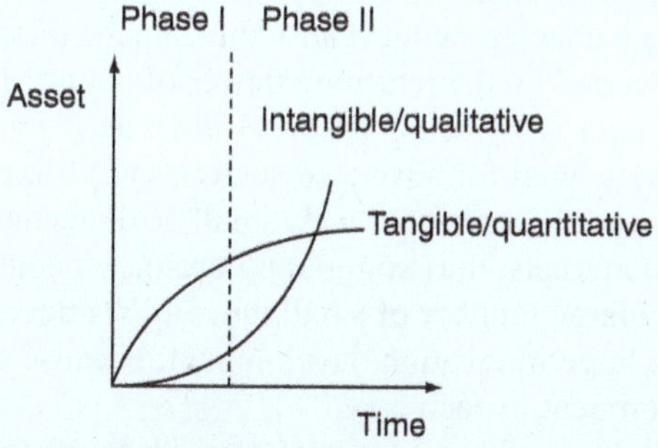

Figure 2.4 From tangible asset growth to intangible asset growth.

and economic development can be positioned in phase I, while development stages in sustainable development mode can be positioned in phase II. Sooner or later, the whole world will have to face up to the requirements of phase II and change its entire growth behavior.

Daly (1996) illustrated this paradigm shift, from phase I to phase II, in two schematic drawings, as shown in Figure 2.5 (a)–(b). That is, Figure 2.5(a) indicates the status of the empty world and Figure 2.5(b) indicates that of the full (saturated) world, treating the economy as an open subsystem of the ecosystem.

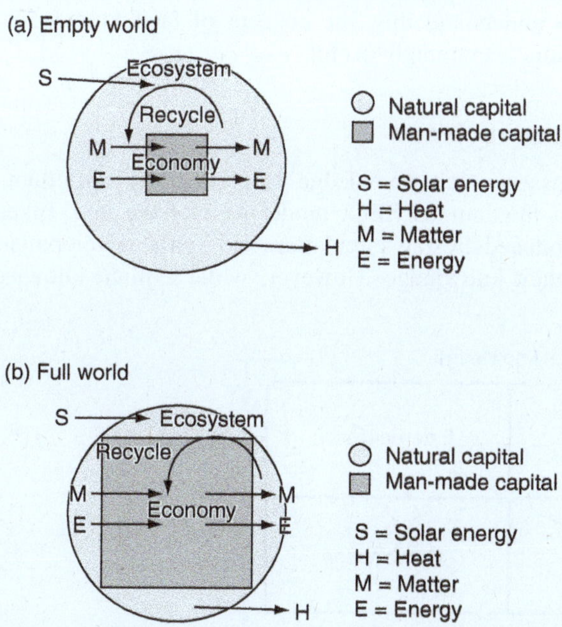

Figure 2.5 The economy as an open subsystem of the ecosystem (source: Daly 1996).

From another economics viewpoint, Schumacher (1973) pointed out that small development is better than large development because the damage of small development can be more readily mended by the returning power of nature.

In his famous book, *Small is Beautiful: A Study of Economics as if People Mattered,* he emphasized that it is beneficial for advanced societies to utilize the somewhat primitive and inexpensive tools associated with small-scale technologies operating in small-scale (niche) markets, thus stimulating ordinary people.

In his context, it is inferred that a large number of small innovations/developments would be better than a single huge innovation/development, because each innovation won't degrade the environment in each case.

Many other economists and sociologists have also presented ideas related to sustainable development issues, including Boyle and Simms (2009), Klein (2007), Latouche (2009), McDonough and Braungart (2002), Savitz and Weber (2006), Pedersen (2009), Lummis (2004) and Senge *et al.* (2008).

As Daly (1997) pointed out, once we recognize the limitations of quantitative economic growth, we have to think about qualitative development. The actual content of qualitative development is understood as a range of intangible assets, such as quality of life, pleasure in community life, satisfaction as consumer, pride in or self-identification with work, brand value, tacit knowledge, and so forth. Most of those things are difficult to evaluate numerically because they are essentially ambiguous, depending on personal feelings and the inner world of human beings.

Daly (1997) also said that we are going from an "Information Economy" to a "Wisdom Economy." To understand this, the concept of tacit knowledge, as described in the next section, is extremely useful.

2.2 Knowledge management issues

Among many tangible assets, tacit knowledge is particularly important for innovation. According to the famous SECI model by Nonaka and Takeuchi (1995), innovation is produced by the circulation and spiral development of explicit knowledge and tacit knowledge. However, while explicit knowledge,

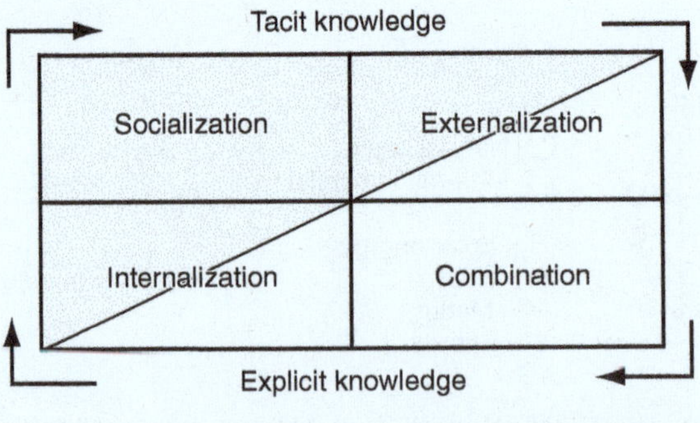

Figure 2.6 SECI model (source: Nonaka and Takeuchi 1995).

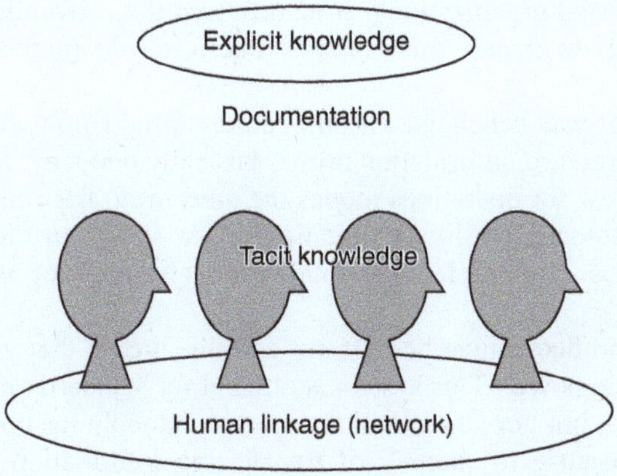

Figure 2.7 Knowledge sharing and human linkage.

such as documentation, patents or information on the Internet, can be transferred outside of human beings, tacit knowledge cannot be transferred without close communication between human beings. Therefore, the management of tacit knowledge through the management of human resources and organization is one of the clues to the qualitative development of current and future society.

According to the SECI model, in order to manage knowledge creation for innovation we need to share both tacit knowledge and explicit knowledge. Explicit knowledge can be shared through documentation as movable information and advances in ICT (Information and Communication Technology), like the internet, have made it freely available across a wide area. However, tacit knowledge is defined as knowledge inside human beings and is not movable. Only by establishing close human links (networks) can it be transferred and shared, as schematically shown in Figure 2.7.

Therefore, establishing human links and human relationships within organizations is an essential element in inducing innovation through sharing and connecting up tacit knowledge. The organization of people and the cultivation of learning inside organizations and between organizations become critically important factors in innovative business in the current world.

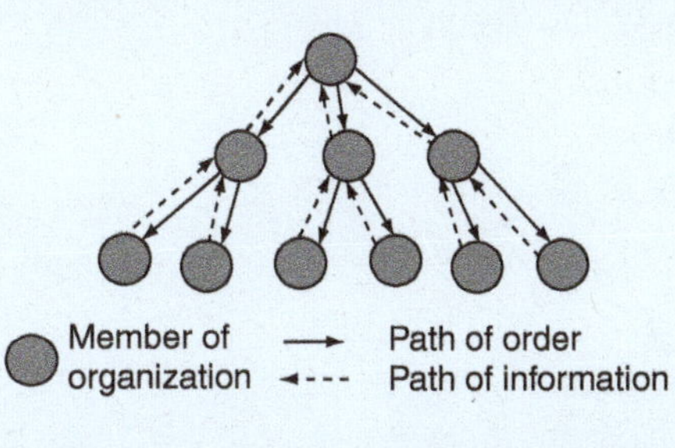

Figure 2.8 Autocratic centralized organization.

The demand for sharing tacit knowledge among people as part of creating innovation changes the preferred organizational structure from the conventional centralized (pyramidal) form to a new autonomous, decentralized (amoebic) form.

The conventional structure was beneficial for unified mass production with a top commander. With that structure, information flow is basically one-way, from bottom to top, while order flow for operations moves the other way, from top to bottom. This resembles an autocratic military organization, as shown in Figure 2.8, because these flows are rational for the totalitarian character of mass production.

In mass production, the products must be uniform and this means they need to be controlled by one central power. This system is rational for standard operations over a long time period, but not so rational for diverse autonomous operations requiring flexibility because its manner of transferring information and ordering is not suitable for intrinsic variety or for quick response to change.

By contrast, the autonomous decentralized structure is rational for non-uniform operations requiring flexibility. It is also suitable for sharing tacit knowledge among many people because information can flow in all directions. Human relationships in this structure are also flexible as the organization is flat and democratic, as shown in Figure 2.9.

As a matter of fact, this new organizational structure is becoming popular in many contemporary industries, particularly the knowledge-based ICT industry.

Based on the discussion in the previous sections, the following three factors can be supposed to be important measures for qualitative sustainable business development in the present era:

1 developing potential new resources and recycling existing natural resources in order to establish businesses with brand competence across a variety of niche markets;
2 creating and developing intangible assets such as regional culture, community solidarity, human vitality and other forms of social capital;

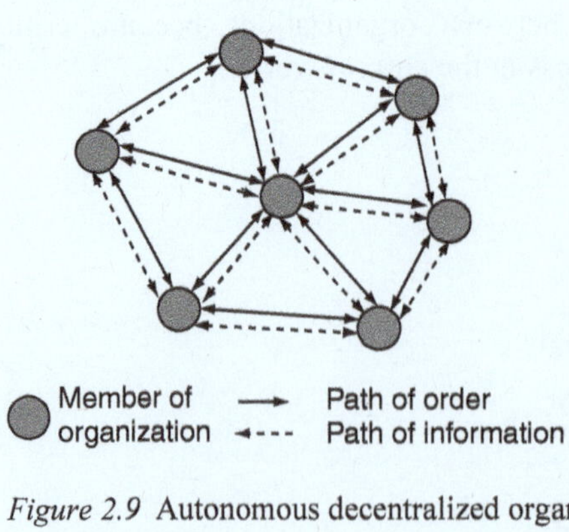

Figure 2.9 Autonomous decentralized organization.

3 creating, sharing and developing tacit knowledge through human linkage for innovation by forming social networks alongside information networks.

It is these factors that will guide the analysis of the many cases of regional enterprise described in later chapters.

2.3 Regional development

As mentioned in this chapter, many economists have discussed the style of management of society and industry from a macroscopic viewpoint, but they have not discussed in detail the management style of enterprises/businesses from a microscopic viewpoint. In many remote, resource-poor stagnated regions, people do not have sufficient business or industrial resources to form industrial clusters or take part in industrial collaboration. For such areas, conventional means of economic development may not be useful. This book focuses on the reality of managing enterprises, including many small and medium enterprises, in Japanese rural regions.

The characteristics of these enterprises will be empirically researched and analyzed in order to obtain useful ideas for many other contemporary enterprises, through characterizing the concrete detail of sustainable-type, or ecological-type, business innovation.

3 Research framework

3.1 Objects of research, standpoint of research

For this book, a number of small and medium enterprises in rural regions in Japan were selected as objects of research. Japan is typical of countries which are experiencing rapid depopulation and aging and its economy has been stagnated for a long time. Over the last couple of decades, regional disparity has become a particularly serious social issue, with many rural villages facing a crisis of collapse. Ironically, many people feel that the government policy of deregulation to encourage industrial development accelerated this regional disparity. In other words, Japan is not unusual in there being many contradictions and problems associated with its attempts to achieve social sustainability.

Interestingly, in another way, Japanese culture seems to have a measure of respect for sustainability in enterprise management. Because of its isolation from other countries by the surrounding sea, Japan has an island culture. Living on an island develops a collaborative rather than a fighting culture because the country is too small for people to fight with each other. In addition, some people say that rice agriculture grows a culture of collaboration because the planting of rice is a collaborative act. Japanese people are sometimes described as having a group-oriented (rather than individualistic) mentality. We don't know the precise origin of such a mentality, but many Japanese do agree that we have a tendency to avoid aggressive conflict within the community. Respect for one another, employees and customers, and caring about social reputation, credibility and loyalty lead the tendency to favor long-term survival of enterprises over generation of large profit in the short term. In Japan, there are numerous long-term (more than one hundred years old) enterprises, known as "shinise [old]" enterprises. Many shinise enterprises don't like rapid growth, or even large profit; they prefer family-like relationships between employees, lifetime employment systems, long-term relationships with customers, and long-term stable development. Many of them have a sustainability-oriented management style. This is extremely interesting from a cultural anthropology viewpoint. Although some people have pointed out that these characteristics indicate the immaturity of capitalism in Japan, the argument is made more complex by the diversity of cultural backgrounds involved and the particular history of Japan.

The author identified a number of businesses in rural parts of Japan which lent themselves to sustainable development, and observed that these businesses were all strongly connected to their regional communities. This might suggest that sustainable development will tend to be associated with a strong sense of community.

In many respects, given that our research purpose is to look at the sustainability of society and business, Japan makes an excellent field of study.

Interestingly, innovation for sustainable development as discussed in the previous chapter is already found in many resource-poor rural regions. The reason is that these regions lack conventional business resources such as investment capital, natural resources such as oil or other precious minerals, or advanced technologies associated with microbiology or the semiconductor industry. Consequently, people in many rural regions have to develop their own business resources by utilizing intangible assets, recycling waste materials, adding value to existing goods, or finding value in something already part of their daily lives. They are not destroying but re-utilizing or recycling 'nature', and maintaining their natural environment because the natural resources around them are so limited. Such innovation cannot be said to be huge or dramatic but, precisely for that reason, it contains some interesting suggestions for the thinking around sustainable development.

Regional development issues are generally discussed in the context of social security issues or related to political management focusing on the industrial/economic development of regions. However, those discussions sometimes restrict the framework of argument into the conventional context of innovation. To develop a new aspect of the discussion, the author would like to propose that we think of regional development issues as clues which could help solve the more universal issue of innovation – that is, help in the search for a new type of innovation to enable contemporary enterprises to survive in the hard competitive environment of a globalized twenty-first century.

3.2 Research question and hypothesis

Our major research question is how to characterize innovation for sustainable development in the current and future world. At the end of Chapter 2, the following three factors were hypothesized to be key elements of such innovation:

1 developing potential new resources and recycling existing natural resources in order to establish businesses with brand competence across a variety of niche markets;
2 creating and developing intangible assets such as regional culture, community solidarity, human vitality and other forms of social capital;
3 creating, sharing and developing tacit knowledge through human linkage for innovation by forming social networks alongside information networks.

In order to explore this hypothesis, a number of regional enterprises will be observed and analyzed.

3.3 Research methodology

The research in this book is mainly empirical and qualitative, based on case studies which enable the in-depth analysis of complex phenomena leading to meaningful insights. At the stage when objective phenomena are complex and dominant parameters to understand the mechanism not yet extracted, the research method of empirical study through cases is more effective than quantitative, statistical methods. To identify the key mechanism of phenomena, detailed description and careful analysis of single cases are particular important.

In total, over twenty cases in Japan are studied in order to analyze the essence of successful contemporary regional businesses in terms of characterizing sustainable-type innovation. The focus on case studies will help readers think about regional issues and sustainable-type innovation very concretely, which will help in sharing the significance of the research with people who are searching for an effective style of business for the future.

3.4 Framework and flow of research

The framework and flow of research in this book are summarized in Figure 3.1.

The internal conditions for establishing a business:
1st step: Human vitality
Social/emotional through art (Chapter 4)
2nd step: Ideas
Creating ecological businesses (Chapter 5)

⇩

The external conditions for establishing a business:
1st step: Community power
Regional community as business platform (Chapter 6)
2nd step: Community design
Sustainable development through community design (Chapter 7)
3rd step: Opening up community
Globalization for regional enterprises (Chapter 8)

⇩

Learning from the above research:
An experiment in regional development (Chapter 9)

⇩

Summary of discussions and conclusions (Chapter 10)

Figure 3.1 Framework and flow of research.

4 Social and emotional development through art

4.1 Introduction

Regional development activities through art and art events can impact in a very special way on regional communities. This will be quite different from the effect of, for example, promoting local industry by inviting large manufacturing factories to the region.

Because art affects people's feelings or sense of spirituality, it can produce emotional development – for example, building a sense of solidarity in a regional community or a passion for the social activities of a regional people.

This chapter looks at the unusual activities of the Seashore Museum in the Japanese city of Kuroshio, obtaining statistical data from questionnaires and qualitative information by interviewing people to show how it has served the region. The results show clearly that the museum's activities have stimulated and improved the self-image of people in the region for over twenty years. Because the concept of the Seashore Museum is based on regional self-confidence, its style of work is currently spreading into regions in other countries such as Mongolia, Brazil and the US (Hawaii). Through its events, the local community of Kuroshio has concomitantly been opened up to the global world.

The other case of stimulus and motivation through art described in this chapter is the Echigo Tsumari Art Triennial held in Niigata Prefecture. With this case, the art events held over three months in a mountainous area called Tsumari attract more than 500,000 visitors and have helped to make the people of the region feel both more confident and more alive. In this case, too, the regional community has been opened up to foreigners and the outside world.

To return to regional issues, many rural regions have problems not only of economic stagnation but also of depopulation, aging, and dispiritedness caused by the falling profitability of agriculture/fishing and a sluggish tourism industry. As well as the direct consequences of economic depression in the regions, emotional/mental depression has become a major obstacle to regional community development.

Matsui and Yamagami (2006) have pointed out that a program called One Village One Product (OVOP) has had some success in bringing some advantage to resource-poor regional people. It was initiated in Oita Prefecture in 1979, the idea being to develop one item as a special product of the locality and be a realistic and effective way of stimulating stagnated regions. The program has rescued many villages without any obvious business resources, the development of their own speciality food or craft items being relatively easy to initiate and to participate in. Because of its practical character, the scheme has spread into other countries in Asia and Africa. One example is the One Tambon One Product (OTOP) program in Thailand; there are other examples in Malawi and in Bayankhongor in Mongolia.

These cases indicate the importance of motivating regional people as a crucial first step in the development of weak rural regions. Because people who have been in a poor economic state for a long time are emotionally depressed, the first step to change the situation is particularly significant. Even if the economic effect of the initial measure is not large, the experience of advantageous change will make people feel more positive and thus vitalized for future progress.

This chapter focuses on regional development through art, examining how different this is from the ordinary process of development. Its aim is to find out the best way to support regional people emotionally and mentally and encourage regional communities to advance themselves.

The first research object is the Seashore Museum in Kuroshio on Shikoku Island. This museum was established in an unusual way with only one million yen (around US$12,000) and its success offers some insight into what is important in the process of regional advance.

The major research question in this chapter is how can art effectively contribute to regional and community development. Careful observation and analysis of the case will indicate some possible answers.

4.2 The case of the Seashore Museum – inexpensive regional museum

4.2.1 Outline of the case

The Seashore Museum in Koroshio on Shikoku island was established in 1989, with a budget of only one million yen (approximately US$12,000). The people of the region were looking to have their own museum, but the area was so poor that an expensive institution was out of the question. It was thought a miracle that a local museum could be constructed on such a restricted budget, because the more usual cost would be at least several hundred million yen.

The trigger behind its establishment was the desire by a photographer in Tokyo to hold an exhibition on Shikoku island. A designer named Makoto Umebara suggested that he silk-screen print his photographs on T-shirts and hang the T-shirts on ropes stretched between poles on the Kuroshio seashore. Because no fine building was required for this "gallery", it could be realized for very little cost.

Umebara and other interested parties, including regional town officers and young people associated with regional development as volunteers, discussed the idea of a "Seashore Museum" as a symbol of development. They talked about how it would exhibit the beauty of the region itself, and turn anything in the region into beautiful artwork. The footprints of birds on the sand, the sight of a whale jumping on the horizon, driftwood on the seashore – all could be interpreted as artworks of a regional nature. They saw the museum as a perfect device for exhibiting the beauty of the region and the seashore in Kuroshio as a perfect place to show how all things in the region are beautiful.

Consequently, they installed the T-shirt exhibition on the seashore and called it a Seashore Museum event.

They advertised the museum as follows: "We don't have a museum in our city. The beautiful seashore is our museum. If we change our way of seeing, we can produce new thinking. If we make our seashore of four kilometers a museum of the mind, we will get many new creative ideas. For example, the beautiful pinewoods become an artwork, the whales jumping in the sea become an artwork, the shallot flowers on the seashore become an artwork, the sea turtles laying eggs on the beach become an artwork, the barefoot children running on the beach become an artwork, the drifts on the beach become an artwork, the patterns of sand made by waves and wind become an artwork, the footprints of small birds on the sand become an artwork, and so on."

The T-shirt exhibition is only one of the events held at the Seashore Museum, and others include an exhibition of quilt art, an exhibition of sand art (sculptures made from the seashore sands), and an exhibition of driftwood. This unique museum has become very well-known on Shikoku island and throughout Japan, with more than 10,000 people – including people from Tokyo and even from

Figure 4.1 Kurishio's Seashore Museum.

Figure 4.2 Silk-screen-printed T-shirts hanging on ropes along the seashore.

abroad – visiting every year over the short period of the exhibition (a few days in May). Over 50 percent of visitors have attended more than twice.

4.2.2 The effect of the project

Due to the success of the museum, Kuroshio has become famous and, as a result, many of the region's people feel proud and have been emotionally boosted by the program.

In addition, the concept has been adopted by other countries, including Mongolia, Brazil and the US (Hawaii). In Mongolia, people held two T-shirt exhibitions on grassland. They called them events from a "Grassland Museum," named after the Seashore Museum. In other words, the idea behind the Seashore Museum was recognized in Mongolia as a universal concept for motivating regional people. Its basic message is, "We regional people are beautiful and our region is beautiful, even though the economic situation is not so good. We love our region. Our museum reveals this beauty to us through art." Through the spread of the event idea, the local communities of Kuroshio and part of Mongolia have established a relationship – even a friendship – with each other. The museum's activities have thus opened up the minds of regional people to the outside world.

Some students and graduate researchers at Kochi University studied the effect of the Seashore Museum through questionnaires in 2000, 2001 and 2002. They were mainly interested in whether the economic aspect or the mental aspect was most significant. According to their report, regional people thought the dominant effect of the Seashore Museum was giving the city a prestigious reputation across the whole country. In mental terms, they were extremely pleased that their home place had become nationally famous and popular.

It was an interesting insight into the consciousness and mentality of regional people. In 2010, in order to confirm the stability of or identify any change in this result, we decided to follow a similar statistical approach, adding interviews with the key people associated with the program.

Our research was conducted at the T-shirt exhibition in Kuroshio over the whole course of the event, May 1–5. The questionnaire was given to randomly selected visitors, ninety in total. The rate of answering was 95 percent and the answers of eighty-five people were collected. The result of the questionnaire is described as follows.

1 Effect of activities

Question: In what way is the Seashore Museum most effective? Please select the main effect from the following options: (1) advancing the reputation of Kuroshio; (2) revitalization of regional people; (3) educating the younger generation in the region; (4) stimulating industry and the economy; (5) other.

Result:

1 reputation: 51 percent
2 revitalization: 32 percent
3 education: 4 percent
4 industry/economy: 2 percent
5 other: 0 percent
6 void: 11 percent

To the question "How large is the effect on regional reputation? Please select the level as, very large, large, medium, small, very small," responders answered: very large 42 percent, large 54 percent, medium 1 percent, small 1 percent, very small 0 percent. In other words, most people thought that the Seashore Museum was effective in significantly enhancing the reputation of the region.

The residence area of responders was analyzed in relation to the above question, with all the people living in Kuroshio positively agreeing on the factor of reputation. It can be concluded, therefore, that the regional people think that the program is effective in advancing the reputation of the city, and they seemed to be proud of it.

The research by Kochi University ten years previously indicated the same tendency. This suggests that the regional people's thoughts and feelings in this respect have been stable and that the program has been effective in developing regional pride and confidence through advancing the reputation of the city.

It makes it clear that local people had not expected to stimulate industry or receive financial advantage from the scheme. They continued to support it for twenty years simply because it was emotionally satisfying.

Because the questionnaire listed revitalization and the stimulation of industry separately, responders were prompted to understand revitalization as different from the stimulation of industry, with revitalization having more spiritual or emotional connotations.

Thus, the results suggest that people think that the program has not so far been effective in prompting industrial development or increasing the income of regional people.

The age of the responders was analyzed in relation to the above question, with the majority of responders selecting the reputation of Kuroshio as the main effect being in their twenties or thirties. This generation has grown up during the Seashore Museum movement, and the fact that it has continued for twenty years might be responsible for this result.

2 Hometown Attachment

Question: How strong are your hometown feelings? Please select the level as: very strong, strong, medium, weak, very weak?

Result:

1 very strong: 72 percent
3 medium: 20 percent
4 weak: 5 percent
5 very weak: 1 percent
6 void: 2 percent

In this case, the fact that most of the responders came from the countryside rather than from a metropolitan area like Tokyo might affect the above result, because urban people do not usually have strong hometown feelings.

Seventy percent of responders were living in Kochi prefecture or on Shikoku island, so that most were local people.

Additional question: What is the dominant factor in developing the attachment to your homeplace?

Result:

1 friendship with local people: 36 percent
2 family or relatives: 27 percent
3 friendship with people living outside the town: 7 percent
4 joining in the activities of regional development: 7 percent
5 other: 5 percent
6 void: 18 percent

The question of the residence area of the responders was also analyzed in relation to the above question, with 76 percent of those living in Kuroshio positively agreeing the factor of reputation.

The results indicate that hometown feelings are not developed through regional revitalization activities like the Seashore Museum but rather through communication with local people. We examined this tendency via another study, interviewing people who moved from a metropolitan area to the regions. To the question about the reason why they moved from an urban area to a rural area, most of them answered that they were attracted by the warmth and simplicity of local people. That is, the most important factor in producing attachment to place was the attractiveness of local people.

4.3 The case of the Echigo Tsumari Art Triennial – impressive regional art event

4.3.1 Outline of the case

The Echigo Tsumari Art Triennial has been held since 2000, with the fourth event held in the autumn of 2009.

The trigger for the event was a prefectural government project named the New Niigata Village Creation Plan, which aimed at regional development through the collaboration of numerous scattered villages in a mountainous area. The project was linked to a bigger project called the Echigo Tsumari Art Necklace Maintenance Project.

The prefectural government invited Fram Kitagawa, a well-known art director born in the prefecture, to promote the project. Mr Kitagawa took the initiative to introduce the idea that "Nature connotes human." Based on this concept he established a whole image for the project around increasing population exchange, getting publicity, and the regional development of an under-populated area in Niigata prefecture.

The project was designed as a temporary subsidized program running from 1996 to 2006, with the main event a triennial exhibition. The first exhibition was held in 2000 and attracted around 160,000 visitors. The second exhibition was held in 2003, attracting some 200,000 visitors, and the third held in 2006 attracted around 350,000 visitors. As will be described later, an extended exhibition was run voluntarily in 2009, attracting over 500,000 visitors.

The events became famous because of their scale. Over one million people have been induced to visit the remote, underpopulated, mountainous region of Niigata as a result of this project, and its example has made many recognize that regional development through art can be enormously effective.

Some 80,000 local people joined in the initial preparatory process, and in doing so discovered for themselves the uniqueness and charm of their area. The regional government supported the decoration of towns with flowers, the maintenance of important buildings to reflect their regional character, and construction projects connected to the exhibition.

The procedure governing the execution of artworks and exhibitions is as follows.

1 The executive committee of the project appeals to the public in the name of the triennial exhibition. Applicant artists submit their artwork and installation proposals.

2 Mr Kitagawa, as art director, selects the artworks for exhibition and announces the content of the plan to communities around the proposed site, inviting any questions they might have for the artists.
3 If the regional people accept the plan, the area for the installation of the artwork is fixed and detailed.
4 The selected artists then initiate the making of their artwork. In many cases, people in the neighborhood of the installations actively support the artists' working.

The collaboration between the artist and regional communities described in the last point is believed to produce a kind of mental integration. As a result, the artist is said to make naturally an artwork which embodies the particular character of regional nature and the lives of regional people.

The role played by volunteers in the project should be also noted. The majority of the volunteers who supported the project were young art students called "Kohebi" (a small regional snake). During the third exhibition of 2006, the number of registered volunteers reached 930, while the total volunteer force was around 2000. These volunteers initially faced opposition from local people who did not understand the intention of the project. They made a great effort to convince regional communities to join in, however, and their perseverance finally generated strong links and feelings of solidarity. When an earthquake happened in the Niigata area latter on, these young volunteers sped to the regions to help and further strengthened their connections.

At the start, the project was met with very severe resistance from the region. Volunteers spent two years trying to convince people of its potential benefit. Eventually the people of the region recognized the stagnated situation they were in and accepted the challenge to try and change it.

One reason for the opposition was that the project was based on *art* and therefore strange and unusual for them. However, their minds started to change when the first exhibition was awarded a home-town events Prime Minister's prize. This inspired self-confidence and was motivational: by the time of the second exhibition, people were more willing to join in. In addition, seeing how many visitors came to their remote region made them recognize the economic potential of the project. Even in the neighboring area of Echigo Tsumari, people was surprised by the number of tourists visiting in the off-season and appreciated the benefit to the regional economy. Consequently, by the end of the third exhibition in 2006, many regional people, as well as the regional hotel union, hoped that the project would continue.

According to the interviews of various people in the region, the affections of the project are summarized in three standpoints of industry (private sector), government (public sector) and regional people (community sector) as follows.

1 Regional tourism operators and people involved in regional industries were impressed by the number of visitors – which exceeded expectations – and the economic effect.

2 The regional municipalities were encouraged by success of the project and the wider area collaboration it promoted became a basis for the future merging of communes.
3 Most of the regional people were initially embarrassed by the project. However, due to the companionable experience of co-working with visiting artists and stimulated by meeting with numerous urban tourists, they recovered their self-confidence and mental liveliness.

At the same time, many visiting artists were stimulated by exchanges with regional people, and they came to be attracted by and sympathetic to the nature of the region and the lives of its people. It is noteworthy too that the people's new sense of solidarity extended to the visiting artists, and thus made the regional community stronger and more open to the outside world.

Throughout these series of exhibitions, certain regional people became interested in the art itself, and took the initiative to make their own artworks. By the fourth exhibition, some individuals applied for a place in the exhibition and were successfully selected as exhibiting artists.

4.3.2 Effect of the project

The project has been hugely subsidized by the Niigata prefecture. Over the ten years of the project, around 600 million yen was spent as subsidy paid by taxation. In addition, there were private donations of around 230 million yen and an income from admission tickets of some 220 million yen. In total, more than one billion yen was spent on the art project for regional development.

The regional government reported that the total economic effect of the project was around 5700 million yen. This estimation included building materials, construction charges and engineering work as part of developing the infrastructure for the event.

They could not expect the fourth exhibition to be subsidized and Souichirou Fukutake, chairman of the Bennese corporation, collected a total of around 300 million yen in private donations. Adding this to the ticket income of some 300 million yen meant that the committee spent more than 600 million yen on the fourth exhibition alone.

It is a very unusual that such a huge budget should be spent on regional development through art. However, because of the enormous value of the economic effect, the project became genuinely sustainable.

As a result of the four exhibitions, a very large number of installed artworks accumulated in the Echigo area. While it is difficult to estimate the monetary value of these accumulated artworks, as intangible assets their value is priceless. The brand value of the region has also been enhanced. The direct plus the indirect economic effect of the art project was extremely large.

4.4 Analysis and discussion

4.4.1 Analysis for the Seashore Museum

The results of the Seashore Museum questionnaire indicated the following propositions:

1 The dominant effect of the Seashore Museum program has been in "advancing the reputation of Kuroshio" over ten years, and regional people believe the program to be mainly effective in this spiritual sense, rather than in the economic sense represented by the stimulation of industry.
2 Regional people have strong hometown feelings and these feelings have been developed through daily relationships with other people in the region rather than through regional development schemes and their events. The hometown feeling seems to be based on long-term daily relationships with people, not on specific activities.

To further study the attitudes of regional people, five key persons of the Seashore Museum were interviewed in more detail.

In these interviews, they said that the people of Kuroshio had been proud of themselves and their regional culture before the events of the Seashore Museum. One reason is that they were educated in the importance of self-confidence and respect for regional culture all through primary school and junior high school. Teachers tell students about Akatsuki Kambayashi, who was born and grew up in Kuroshio and became a famous Japanese novelist. He wrote many fine novels in the Meiji period after the modernization of Japan. He said, "A flower lying on the ground is more beautiful than a flower blooming on the branch of the tree," which means, "local culture is more important than urban culture for local people." The people in Kuroshio appreciate this expression and have engraved it on a memorial stone erected on the Kuroshio seashore.

The interviewees indicated that it was education of this sort and its cultural context that developed the regional people, making it an important reason for the Seashore Museum movement continuing so successfully for twenty years.

This implies that some kind of basis of hometown feeling and respect for regional culture needs to pre-exist in regions if the success and continuation of regional development activities are to be enabled.

In this context, the events of the Seashore Museum have had some interesting effects on the local community. Following the organization of the Grassland Museum in Mongolia, the pupils of Kuroshio elementary school formed a relationship with their pupil counterparts in Mongolia, and they have started to develop friendships through the exchange of pictures and other items. In the past, there was a culture of respect for regional people, but no interaction with other regional peoples. The Seashore Museum movement has also spread to Hawaii and to Brazil. Through events associated with this proliferation, the local community of Kuroshio has been opened up to local communities in other countries. Art activities have opened the window of globalization.

4.4.2 Analysis of the Echigo Tsumari Art Triennial

The impact on the regional people and the artists of this project is summarized as follows.

1 Many regional people were stimulated by and gained confidence from the experience of companionship and co-working with visiting artists.
2 By looking at the artwork through which the artists expressed their sympathy for a region's natural environment and the human lives in it, regional people learn to understand the power of art. Some initiated their own artworks. Through contact with artworks, people in the region could explore their own responses and increase their self-confidence.
4 By joining the project, they felt a sense of achievement and the joy of participation. Their self-confidence was enhanced by the activities themselves and by the collaborative experience, linked to a feeling of self-identity.
4 Through exchanges with the numerous tourists from urban areas, they felt stimulated and emboldened.
5 The economic benefits resulting from the project made people feel more positive about taking on new challenges.

In general, these different opportunities and processes made the people of the region feel more alive and positive.

With the exception of the economic effect, most of these effects were similarly observed with the Seashore Museum, and even in Tsumari, most of the people in remote mountainous areas were not affected by the economic impact of the project. The economic effect is mostly seen in the construction, tourism, hotel and restaurant, and transport industries. But although most people in mountainous areas did not see much benefit of this sort, the project nevertheless served to inspire them.

According to the statistical data from the questionnaires given to the sixty-one members of the event's executive committee in 2006, 90 percent of responders felt that the events had vitalized the region (strongly: 49 percent, somewhat: 41 percent).

Using a multi-selection answering system, responses to the question about what aspect of the region had been vitalized were (1) the activities of communities were enhanced: 63 percent; (2) the sightseeing resources and attractions of the region were improved: 56 percent; (3) the cities were stimulated by visitors: 46 percent, (4) the cultural environment was enhanced: 37 percent; (5) sales in the shops were increased: 24 percent; and "other": 20 percent.

Thus, most people felt that the events had vitalized the region intellectually and culturally rather than economically.

4.4.3 Comparative analysis of the two cases

In the case of the Seashore Museum in Kuroshio, the economic effect of events is relatively limited, at least at the current stage. Even though there were more than 10,000 visitors to the T-shirt exhibition over a few days, direct effects in economic terms is still small.

According to the research carried out by Kochi University between 1999 and 2001, which involved questioning thirteen residents in Kuroshio, the majority answered that the most outstanding effect of the events was the improvement of the city's image. The other effects of the events were thought to be mental stimulus and interest in education; only a few people answered that there was an economic effect.

Thus, art events for regional development could produce significant intellectual or cultural effects for regional people, even though they might not have a strong economic impact.

One reason for such effects might be the fact that many regional people are engaged in agriculture, fishing and allied industries and, generally lacking the opportunity to make connections with the outside world and its people, are particularly stimulated by the events. Exchanges with volunteers, artists, and visitors from elsewhere might serve to activate regional people and boost the spirits of those with uneventful daily lives.

Art is not about commercial profit but about personal catharsis or the satisfaction of expressing oneself. Some contemporary artists are pursuing exchanges with society as a way of expressing oneself. In such instances, certain artists intentionally install their artworks in public places, while others make their artworks in deliberate collaboration with ordinary people. Some artists seem to think that the act of collaborating with ordinary people is in itself an artwork. They seem to be aiming to describe feelings of human alienation from society or feelings around the recovery of solidarity with a community. Some artists say that the purpose of contemporary art is to criticize human behavior/society. It is interesting that artworks on show affected local people emotionally, whatever the artists' intention might have been.

One thing that we have to think of here is the goal or purpose of regional people. With reference to the pursuit of happiness, people in the regions sometimes say that their ultimate aim is not economic improvement but rather a satisfying community life or a lifestyle in harmony with nature.

The two cases in this chapter show that the purpose of regional people's activities was not only economic improvement and the correction of regional disparity but also some less tangible things. Nevertheless, some kind of economic basis is important for any activity, even if it is an art activity.

Economic improvement and mental uplift are not alternatives, not even antinomies. They can be harmonized and synergetic, and balanced to complement each other.

In the cases here, the scale of the budgets was very different. With the Echigo Tsumari Triennial, a very large budget was supported by subsidy and its economic effect was also very large. With the Seashore Museum, in contrast, the total budget was extremely small – especially for the first event – and its economic effect was also small. But even the Seashore Museum needed a small amount of money. In fact, the local government is currently supporting the museum with a budget of around fifty million yen per year because its activities have been extended to many areas of public service. In both cases, therefore, an appropriate budget was essential.

The reality is that adequate financial basis and spiritual/emotional effects are linked, and if one is lacking, the other cannot be advanced. For this reason, the collaboration of private, public and community elements, as well as consensus within communities, is essential for any progress.

In every region, some people particularly value the economic element, while others value the less tangible mental element. Thus, a regional people's collective decision regarding what they are aiming at will be particular to the region, and every region's development methodology will also be different.

In reality, there would be numerous arguments around such matters as, "Is it beneficial for the region or not, to pursue economic prosperity by destroying the region's natural environment and building a huge tourism centre in the town?" and "After achieving economic prosperity, village people lost their communal solidarity and peaceful atmosphere."

In projects of regional development through art, these kinds of contradictions and conflicts arise particularly, because of the characteristics of art. It is usually difficult to evaluate the economic effect of art events, and some people are therefore skeptical about the merit of vitalizing projects involving art. Regional people are being asked what is the purpose of these projects and what they hope to gain from them.

4.5 Conclusion

The Seashore Museum is a unique example of regional development. Instead of building a large physical museum, the people of Kuroshio on Shikoku island set up an exhibition in the form of T-shirts on ropes along the seashore. Because of the low cost and particular character of the museum, it was easy for regional people to initiate, participate in, and continue. This achievability, plus the elements which prompted people to respect and be proud of themselves, made it of interest to other rural areas and the concept has been successfully transferred elsewhere, even into other countries.

To clarify the effect of the scheme on the region's people, a statistical study by questionnaire and a qualitative study through interviews were carried out.

The results of the questionnaire indicated the following:

1 The dominant effect of the Seashore Museum movement has been "advancing the reputation of Kuroshio", and regional people have mainly seen the movement as effective in this spiritual area, not in economic ways such as the stimulus of industry.

2 Regional people have a strong feeling of hometown and this feeling has grown up through interaction with their fellows and not through regional development projects. The hometown feeling seems to be based on long-term daily relationship with people, not on specific activities.

In addition, the results of the interviews indicate that the basis of the hometown feeling and respect for regional culture needs to be historically established in regions before the onset of regional development projects in order for them to be successful and continue. This suggests that some kind of pre-existing basis of regional culture may need to be present for successful development schemes, even if their form is readily accessible.

In the case of the Echigo Tsumari Triennial, the following points were observed to be similar to the case of the Seashore Museum.

1 Many regional people were stimulated through companionship and co-working with the visiting artists.
2 By looking at the artworks through which the artists expressed their sympathy for the natural environment of the region and human lives, regional people recognized the power of art. Some people initiated their own artworks. People made up their own minds about the works of art and became more self-confidence.
3 By joining the project, people felt the joy of the activities themselves and a sense of achievement. Their self-confidence was enhanced through participation in the activities and in project collaborations, linked to a developing self-identity.
4 Through exchanges with numerous tourists from urban areas, people were stimulated and grew more confident.
5 The economic impact of the project made people feel more alive and more ready to take on new challenges.

The Echigo Tsumari Triennial had a substantial subsidised budget and its economic effect was substantial. Even art events require an appropriate budget. The economic basis and spiritual/emotional effect are linked together, and if one of them is lacking, the other cannot advance. This prompted the collaboration of the private sector, public sector and regional community.

The two cases indicate that we can establish small projects without huge expense and also that we can establish big projects with big budgets. Both ways can work. For most resource-poor rural regions, projects without too much expense are the more realistic. For this reason, the Seashore Museum program has spread to other countries.

Regional development through art has the potential to boost regional people emotionally and intellectually, and communities in the regions can also be made more open to outsiders though art events. Even for regions which lack good business resources, art can be seen as a useful development tool.

The spread of the art events elsewhere has connected regional communities to the local communities of other countries. In this way, art activities have given them a new global perspective.

Future studies should pursue the precise conditions for the effectiveness of programs of this kind in order to find more universal solutions for the problems of regional disparity and regional depression.

Acknowledgments

The author would like to express his sincere thanks to the interviewees who provided information about the Seashore Museum, including Kentarou Murakami, Toshirou Matsumoto, Taira Yasumitsu, Yasuhiro Nonoshita, Ms Kaori Toyama, and Makoto Umehara.

Thanks are also due to the many supporters of the statistical study, including Atsushi Shoujima, Natsuki Shiozaki, Masafumi Takemura and Fusano Akahori.

The author would also like to express his appreciation to the interviewees who provided information about the Echigo Tsumari Art Triennial, including Suzanne Klien, Katsuyoshi Takahashi, Masanori Watanabe, Makoto Sakai and Fumito Watanuki.

This research was supported by the budget for the Strategic Collaboration among Universities for Regional Issues project, financed through the Japanese government's Ministry of Education, Culture, Sports, Science and Technology.

5 Creating ecological businesses

5.1 Introduction

Many small, resource-poor regions in many countries have been getting increasingly poor, depopulated, elderly and devitalized. For example, in Japan, the population of many villages and towns, in mountain areas and on islands, has fallen to less than 2000. In addition, the proportion of people over sixty-five has increased by over 50 percent in many regions. These regions are called "marginal," which means that their ability to survive has reached its limit. The social cost of a region's vital infrastructure – its water supply, electricity, roads, and so on – increases dramatically if the total population of the region is less than 2000.

In such areas, sustainable innovation is needed. In rural regions which lack conventional business resources such as capitalization, natural assets or advanced technology, people need to develop their own business resources by creating value in resources considered valueless in a conventional context. That is, they need to recycle items from daily life, or develop a new usage for garbage. In addition, to make a difference, these kinds of innovatory practices need to continue in a region over a long time period. This chapter looks at and analyzes several business cases in rural parts of Japan to try and identify the characteristics of such sustainable innovation and arrive at universal principles which might be relevant for other resource-poor regions in the world today.

The first case is a business selling leaves in mountains, the second a business selling wood shavings, and the third a business selling misshapen citrus fruit which cannot be sold on the commercial market. All these cases are found in mountain villages on the island of Shikoku in Japan. In these businesses cases, village people have spent many years and much effort on marketing, on improving commercial items as part of developing a new business model, and on creating new business resources to compensate for the shortage of conventional business resources. Moreover, they involve older people in mountain villages. In these villages, the traditional industries such as forestry and horticulture have declined because of cheap imports from abroad or natural disasters, and this has accelerated the departure of the young. This adds to the depression of local businesses and the low morale of those who remain – it is a vicious circle. The new businesses described in this chapter are reversing this trend.

All their activities are successful in maintaining natural resources and not damaging the ecology and are thus sustainable. For this reason, innovation of this kind may be usefully adapted to disadvantaged regions in other parts of the world.

Concerning marketing, branding has been an extremely important factor in their success. As a result of globalization, many rural regions in Japan have lost their competitive industrial competence because of the emergence of countries with lower labor cost and spillover technologies. Not only in manufacturing industries but also in primary industries such as agriculture, forestry and fishery, many enterprises have lost their competitive advantage. Some manufacturing businesses have survived by shifting their production bases to the emerging countries; however, the same strategy cannot be used with primary industries because their production bases are too closely connected to particular places. In order to try and overcome the problems of regional industries, one idea is to make as much as possible of the locality. That is what is called a regional branding strategy. To emphasize the characteristics of a locality, marketing people establish a regional brand.

The strategy of the first three cases in this chapter is just this strategy of regional branding: one business emphasized the advantages of a riverside lifestyle, while emphasized the benefits of a mountain lifestyle. Both cases had promoted their regional brand by emphasizing the value of a natural life in the regions. Through this branding strategy, their products were imbued with the priceless qualities of a natural life in the countryside and thus became attractive to urban consumers.

Using this idea, other products have been created without expensive resources. The fourth case described below is a business which makes use of dialect, the fifth case is a business involving local carts, the sixth case is a business selling local alcoholic drinks, vinegar, and cosmetics. These businesses took inexpensive resources in the regions and developed them into a regional brand. The thinking could be followed by many regions stagnated by globalization.

How to stimulate economically stagnated/depressed regions and how to develop competitive industry in the regions is a significant issue for the government of Japan, as well as for governments in other countries.

To return to the history of economics management, industrial clustering was proposed as one way to encourage development in the regions. That is, the strength of each separate enterprise in a region was thought to be enhanced by regional clustering. Marshall (1890) pointed out the economic effect of the "geometrical" integration of enterprises from the viewpoint of reduced costs of production, more rational logistics and economies of scale. Many researchers (for example, Anzoff 1965 and Krugman 1991) developed the theory by focusing on the synergy effect and cost reduction of clustering. In the decade of the 1990s, Porter (1990) pointed out the importance of knowledge integration. His focus was on how the synergy effect of accumulating, combining and sharing varieties of knowledge leads to innovation, as in Silicon Valley in the US. His theory also indicated that sharing tacit knowledge through regional human networks is key for both innovation and the competitive core competence of enterprises, alongside the sharing of explicit knowledge through information networks.

The importance of tacit knowledge in innovation was pointed out by Badaracco (1991) and Nonaka and Takeushi (1995). They described the characteristics of knowledge links and circulation, identifying two kinds of knowledge, one explicit and the other tacit, and argued that combining and sharing these two kinds of knowledge in organizations was the basis of innovation.

Many depressed regions in the current day, however, do not have the basis for competitive industry, neither the advanced technologies of Silicon Valley nor any other significant business resource as a core for clustering. In any case, the development of a single enterprise is not enough to make a difference to a depressed region. Such regions need support and encouragement over a long period to produce new sorts of competitive business.

Innovation means a change in business creation, the introduction of a new idea, resource or tool for establishing a better market environment around an enterprise. How far the market is changed has generally been thought an important factor in evaluating innovation. However, the sustainability of the change and how it impacts on the natural environment is now, or should be, the more important factor, particularly at the present time.

It is interesting, therefore, that just such kinds of sustainable-type innovation are sometimes found in rural regions. Because many rural regions lack conventional business resources (capitalization, natural assets, advanced technology, and so on), rural people have to develop their own business resources by utilizing, recycling, adding value to or finding value in something from their daily lives.

5.2 The case of Irodori – a business selling leaves

The first case is an unusual and rather entertaining business story. It is an account of the Irodori corporation's business of selling leaves in Kamikatsu, a remote mountain village on Shikoku island. The village has a population of around 2000 and more than half the people are over sixty-five years old. In that sense, it is a typical "marginal village" in Japan.

Around twenty years ago, a typhoon damaged the orange farms which were the main industry of the village, and the village people were at a loss what to do. Tomoji Yokoishi, a member of the village agriculture union (a branch of the Japanese Agriculture Union), came up with the idea of selling leaves from the mountains to high-class urban restaurants. Chefs at such restaurants use fresh leaves to decorate luxurious traditional dishes and he thought the village people would have a market.

When they began, few village people believed that it could be a real business which earned money. And as a matter of fact, nobody purchased their leaves at the start. However, Mr Yokoishi did not give up and he spent over ten years on marketing in order to turn their leaves into commercial items. There turned out to be commercial specifications even for leaves. For example, buyers had very specific requirements regarding the quality, features, color, size and thickness of leaves, and they also demanded quantities of leaves with the same qualities, features, color and so on, so they could supply a number of customers at the same time. Delivery time was another issue. Chefs decide their menus in the early morning after seeing what fresh fish and vegetables are available in the market, and need leaves which match the dishes chosen for the evening of the same day. Thus, the leaves need to be received within twelve hours of the order being placed. Mr Yokoishi has visited numerous luxury restaurants as a customer and spent a lot of his own money in order to research the specifications of leaves for the target restaurants. After a long time and a lot of effort, he eventually established how to market leaves from the mountains as commercial items.

In parallel, he also established a suitable supply-chain management system using broadband technology. There is now a very up-to-date information system in the village. Villagers aged eighty and ninety are accessing the internet on computers and getting orders through the system. Because the village is small it is convenient for the rapid transfer of leaves to the business centre in the village, and the collected leaves can then be delivered to the restaurants by air courier service in half a day. Mr Yokoishi devised a homepage set-up which senior citizens could easily use. Before introducing this system, he used fax machines, which are installed in each village home for urgent use, as the basis for supply chain management. He said, "We can use any kind of tool for our idea. The important thing is not the particular technology but using it in our manner."

Nowadays the village people earn an annual total of around 300 million yen (around US$3 million) by selling leaves, and one lady over eighty years old earns more than ten million yen a year just by selling leaves. Interestingly, they can now earn more money by selling the leaves from a persimmon tree than selling the fruits from that same tree. Another benefit is that many senior persons have become healthier and more active as a result of the leaves business, and their healthcare costs have drastically reduced. Mr Yokoishi said, "Every person is needed by everyone. We need to prepare the stage for everyone to be active. The senior persons in this village are important and precious because they are the very persons who know where we can collect the leaves in the village. The younger people cannot find the leaves."

This success story became famous even overseas, and Mr Yokoishi was named as one of the most successful social entrepreneurs in the world by an American business journal.

The most impressive element in this story is that the business was established using existing natural resources and existing human resources, even though neither resource had been thought to have any value. Its business style is sustainable and ecological, with existing resources utilized without any damage to the natural environment. This case indicates a new style of business fit for our survival in the current century.

One important lesson to be learnt from this case is that the establishment of a successful business requires not only identifying the resources but also "growing" them as commercial items through long-term marketing. Even for leaves, marketing proved essential: for any kind of item, marketing will be indispensable to successful commercialization.

5.3 The case of Shimanto Drama – selling the riverside lifestyle

The second case is another unusual business, that of the Shimanto Drama Company selling wood shavings in Kochi prefecture on Shikoku island.

The Shimanto river is considered one of the three most beautiful clear watercourses in Japan. It runs for about 200 kilometers and many villages are located along its course. Shimanto Drama was established in 1994 by three villages along the river. Taisho, Towa and Nishitosa villages each invested eight billion yen to establish a company to support village people's lives. The next year, some individuals purchased this corporation to privatize it completely. Mr Azechi, who was a member of the agriculture union, joined this company as its manager and subsequently spent his whole life developing the business. At the start there were only three employees, but nowadays there are twenty employees and annual sales are worth around 300 million yen.

Their main business is selling agricultural and fish products from the local area. They also decided to process foods through collaborations with village people and opened their own shop selling foodstuffs and souvenirs, named Michi-no-eki Towa, utilizing government support. This shop has turned out to be extremely successful despite its remote location, thought to be so bad for business. Two reasons for its success are the unique and desirable processed foodstuffs it offers and the many devices in the shop designed to attract consumers.

One especially interesting item is a package of wood shavings. There are lots of forests around the villages and village people sell wood from these forests. In particular, Hinoki wood has a good smell and is consequently popular as a material for making wooden bath-tubs. Therefore, Hinoki wood can be sold for a good price in Japan. The wood industry produces a large quantity of wood shavings during its processing operations. Shimanto Drama came up with the idea of selling the wood shavings in a kind of scent bag to be used in the bath. It was thought that, although ordinary people in large cities and metropolitan areas could not afford expensive Hinoki bath-tubs, they could enjoy the smell of Hinoki by purchasing Hinoki wood shavings. They started to sell packages of the shavings for 800 yen and they became very popular. Now they are also selling the shavings through other souvenir shop channels.

The business strategy of Shimanto Drama is quite close to that of Irodori. The focus was always on marketing and promotion. In the early stage of the business they published *Water*. This book was filled with descriptions of the riverside lifestyle along the Shimanto. They asked celebrities from the journalism and art worlds to contribute essays to their book. They said, "We don't have money and we are very poor in the region. But we have very rich nature around the

Shimanto river. We would like to pay your writing fee with fish caught in the Shimanto." Fortunately, many famous artists and writers were interested in their unique proposal and wrote pieces for them. The book was published to promote the value of the river and to brand their region.

They also brought out a seasonal magazine, *Riverside Life,* for circulation to more than a 1000 supporters of the Shimanto Drama business. The purpose was again to promote the value of the riverside lifestyle and help brand their region. The mission of the enterprise is to respect riverside country life and its beautiful natural environment.

Through promotional activities and by using attractive packaging for all their items, they established the value of their products and made them successful. Even when selling wood waste, they added their message of respect for nature and pleasure in country lives.

There is great attention to detail. For example, the shop's bathroom is always cleaned thoroughly and there is a notice saying, "We appreciate your using the bathroom in a clean manner. Because each of you is conscious of the importance of maintaining its cleanliness, the room will always be kept clean and enjoyable. We thank you for your continuing effort." By the accumulation of such small measures they are helping to establish their regional brand.

Concerning products, they continue to develop new items all the time. They know that the creation of new products is one way to attract people. Taking care over packaging and the manner of arranging items in the shop and making point-of-purchase advertising material to provide information to customers, they have added value to their products. These practices are familiar to any retailer. However, the number of regional enterprises which adhere to such principles for business success is not very large.

5.4 The case of Umaji village – selling the mountain lifestyle

The third case is the Umaji village agriculture union business, again in Kochi prefecture on Shikoku island, of selling misshapen citrus fruit (yuzu oranges).

Umaji is another small village in a mountain area, with a population of only around 1000. Thirty-four percent of the village people are over sixty-five years old. In the past, the main industry of the village was selling wood from the mountain forests. However, the price of wood has been drastically reduced by the appearance of inexpensive Asian timber and it has ceased to be a profitable business.

Villagers have also been growing, for fifty years or so, the trees of yuzu, a citrus fruit similar to an orange, and so were keen to sell yuzu fruit instead of wood. However, their yuzu fruit were mostly misshapen and therefore unsuitable to sell in the usual way, because the Japanese consumer does not like to buy misshapen fruit.

They then came up with the idea of making juice and flavorings from the fruit, but it proved difficult, as unknowns, to break into the new market. Mochifumi Toutani, a leader in the agriculture union, then played a key role over the next twenty years in marketing and promoting the products via attractive packaging design, flyers, and a television campaign. His strategy was to develop an image of simple, peaceful lives in a mountain area of great natural beauty, in order to attract urban consumers to the village. And all the products, such as juice, seasonings and wooden bags made in the village, were characterized as part of these peaceful, natural lives. The strategy was very similar to that of Shimanto Drama. It proved equally successful and the company's items have become more popular, receiving awards in rural exhibitions. In addition to promotional activity, they have reduced retailing and logistical costs by utilizing internet sales and direct delivery services.

A good delivery service is essential to the success of internet selling. Similarly to the leaves business in Irodori, the village's adoption of internet-based direct sales was related to the extension of delivery services. When delivery services reached even remote villages, many villages were able to initiate internet-based retail businesses.

Nowadays the business has over eighty employees and its annual sales have reached over three billion yen (roughly $30 million). They have more than 25,000 visitors a year and villagers have become proud of themselves and of their remote village.

They also developed a craft business using thin wooden laminate. The trigger was over ten years ago, when they were making trays from surplus wood. An industrial designer from outside proposed that they make an ecological bag using the same laminated material as the tray. The resultant bags had the very taste of nature and ecology and even became popular overseas. The Museum of Modern Art in New York purchased some, and retail shops in other countries deal with them.

Ecological lifestyle became the main mission of the enterprise and the policy governing their regional business activity. Like Shimanto Drama, they are selling the country lifestyle through their items. Also similarly, regional branding has been a strong business tool and it is not too much to say that they are mostly selling intangible assets rather than products. Utilizing valueless misshapen items, they created value through long-term marketing activity. This is also similar to the business case of Irodori.

5.5 The case of the Life Creation Studio – dialect as business resource

Any intangible asset in regions can be sold and become a seed for business development. This is the story of a business selling regional dialect.

Ms Kae Ohno originally learned information technology and acquired business experience through working for a trading company. Then she got an idea to launch a business utilizing regional dialect as a free resource. She made a version of a traditional Japanese card game called "Karuta." Players use two kinds of card, one kind with an expression in regional dialect and the other kind with the meaning of the dialect expression in standard Japanese. Players have to pair up the cards in regional dialect and standard Japanese. Because the main business resource was regional dialect, the cost of initiating the business was relatively limited.

The idea was unique and interesting. But, just as in the other business cases, she had to expend a lot of effort on the marketing side. In addition, collecting precise dialect expressions was hard work, like an academic research project. Also, gaining credibility for her product was tough, buyers being frequently skeptical about the value of the card game. After these efforts, her card game became popular as a regional souvenir or enjoyable game and she sold several thousand units.

This account tells us that anything can be a resource for business, but just as with the Irodori and Umaji village enterprises, marketing proved essential for producing an item with real commercial value.

5.6 The case of Yubu island – selling the peaceful feeling

Kochi prefecture is sometimes called "the remote island on land." The Yaeyama islands in Okinawa prefecture are sometimes called "the really remote islands in the sea." Both regions are known for their low GDP and low average living standards. Ishigaki is one of the Yaeyama islands, 400 kilometers from Okinawa island. Iriomote is the next island to Ishigaki, and Yubu is a very small island close to Iriomote.

There were no islanders on Yubu before the end of the Second World War. After the war ended, some people began to live on the island, and by 1969, around 180 people were resident there. However, the island was sunk into the sea by a typhoon, and only three families were able to stay. Three years later, there was an idea to establish a botanic garden to stimulate tourism on the island. However, to induce tourists to come to such a tiny island was extremely difficult. One trigger for success was the idea of using a cart pulled by water buffalo as a sightseeing coach for visitors coming from Iriomote island. The sea between the two islands is very shallow and a cart with water buffalo is an amusing transport feature for tourists. A senior driver of the coach guides the water buffalo along while singing a folksong of the region and playing a three-stringed traditional instrument. It makes for a peaceful scene, and many urban tourists are fascinated by the peaceful atmosphere. This experience has became so popular that over 1500 visitors come to Yubu island each day.

Since so many tourists now come to the island, the business was extended into the growing and selling of tropical fruit (mango, pineapple, guava, papaya, and dragon fruit) to tourists, and the making of fruit juices, jellies, and water ices. Employees now number around seventy at the botanic garden and about thirty at the fruit farm.

This business used only resources from the islanders' daily lives, but eventually achieved success. The shallow, unexceptional sea and the ordinary, rather dirty water buffaloes became a major draw for tourists. The essence of the charm they had for urban visitors was the way they represented "peaceful country life."

This case shows us the limits of the usual SWOT (Strengths, Weaknesses, Opportunities, Threats) analysis for business strategy. In normal SWOT analysis, the shallow sea and the slow-moving water buffaloes would be classified as elements of weakness. However, for urban people, they are the strength of the business.

Most of the resources were not in any way special, nor were they thought to have any commercial significance. But by adding an innovative idea to a combination of these "ordinary" elements, they became valuable business assets. In addition, the natural environment was not being destroyed and the business is sustainable.

One aspect of the success of this business is the size of its market, which is niche and small but provides an income which is adequate. If the islanders significantly grew the business and attracted 10,000 or 100,000 visitors a day, the island would be damaged and its charm would be destroyed. Neither sustainable lifestyles nor sustainable business styles can be about the pursuit of major monetary returns. By appropriately limiting the level of profit, both the business and the associated environment can be maintained sustainably. This kind of balance was proposed by Daly (1996) and Schumacher (1973).

This case can be seen to symbolize sustainability, its very simplicity making it easy to understand. Some readers might wonder if it could be a model for people in urban areas. The type of industry and the size of sales and profit will probably be different in an urban area. However, the basic concept can suggest a way of thinking about business that is relevant even for urban people. How to control the size of a business and maintain it at a suitable level is important in all kinds of environment. If we pursue profit as much as far as possible and infinitely follow our desires, there will be problems in the future. This story is easy to understand because its implications are very clear.

5.7 The case of the sake cellar on Ishigaki – an island recycling business

On Ishigaki island, a certain sake cellar is involved in the business of making sake and other alcoholic drinks, vinegar and cosmetics from the natural resources of the region.

This enterprise has annual sales of about 800 million yen (around $8 million) and has some fifty employees. The current head of the business is the son of the founder. He graduated from the University of Agriculture and Technology in Tokyo and is involved in developing new products with his own son.

The new products always use local materials, and this practice is shared with many other sake cellars. In all parts of Japan, sake cellars use the water and rice of the locality. Because of this, the taste of each sake is different depending on the region. On Okinawa and Yaeyama islands, there was no rice suitable for traditional sake. They could get only imported rice, which was different from the usual Japanese rice. So people on Okinawa could not make good sake. However, a distilled alcoholic drink made from this rice proved distinctive and popular.

Okinawa people called this drink “Awamori” to distinguish it from the more traditional Shouchu. As this indicates, every regional sake cellar has a way of creating special products which utilize local materials.

This particular enterprise developed many other unique products, including Habu Sake (a snake-infused sake), pineapple wine (a wine-like drink made from pineapples), and Moromizu (a vinegar made from imported rice). Moromizu was a particular hit and they sold over one million bottles of it one year. But even then, production was deliberately limited and they avoided expansion. The head of the business said, “We know the right level of production. Expansion of the business would not have been a good decision.”

They also developed cosmetics by using fish collagen. Ishigaki is a small island so they could not use material from land animals, but fish were an available resource. Although these manufactured cosmetics were not a great success, during the BSE crisis they were rated highly by some from the point of view of safety and benefit to health.

The management style of this enterprise is respect for employees, because sake is considered to be a living thing and, according to the business owner, the state of mind of the employees affects its taste. Making fine-tasting sake is synonymous with treating employees like members of a real family, he said. The business was run in a traditional Japanese way, with lifetime employment and a promotion system based on seniority. Apart from the issue of whether this is good or bad, most sake cellar businesses have adopted sustainable-type management practices. They are not aiming for drastic growth like J-curb start-ups but rather at steady continuation. They do not like changing the size of their business and prefer maintaining the same level of sales. This attitude seems to be connected to their profound affection for the natural environment of the area.

5.8 Analysis and discussion

The cases examined in this chapter show some similarity in relation to styles of regional development.

1 Recycling and developing resources:
   With all the cases, village people made use of resources which had no value in a conventional context.

   Leaves from trees were not commercial items. Wood shavings were useless waste for throwing away. Misshapen fruit could not be sold. However, Mr Yokoishi of the Irodori corporation persisted with his market research for over ten years to see how leaves might have value, and eventually turned these leaves into successful commercial items. Mr Azechi of the Shimanto Drama Company and Mr Toutani of the agriculture union in Umajimura were also involved in lengthy marketing activities. Their efforts too created new commercial products.

   This production of saleable goods did not damage the natural environment: in all three cases, they used or recycled items normally considered waste. In that sense, the businesses contributed to the ecological maintenance of the Earth.

The people of Kamikatsu, Shimanto and Umaji are noted for their respect for nature. Kamikatsu is famous for its zero-emission program, which aims to recycle all waste materials. People in all three of the regions appear to relish their simple lives in remote villages, spent in harmony with the natural environment.

2 Activating resource-poor people:
The success of the businesses helped to empower marginal people in remote areas. In Kamikatsu, the older generation was particularly affected. In general, people over sixty-five are not expected to make up a valuable labor force because of their physical limitations. However, for Irodori, the older generation turned out to be the best at finding the leaves to meet restaurants' demands because they knew the trees in their local mountains so well. And because leaves are small and light, the elderly can easily handle them. The pleasure of earning their own money and being able to buy things for their families tremendously revitalized the older generation in Kamikatsu, with direct consequences for their health. Healthcare expenses for the elderly in Kamikatsu are now so reduced that the region is famous for having the lowest such costs in Japan.

People connected to Shimanto Drama and the enterprise in Umaji have also been very much stimulated by their business success. Shimanto Drama has set up a club called "River" and produced a periodical to describe the pleasures of life along the Shimanto river. They have also published "A Book of Water", with articles on the theme by eminent artists, writers, and novelists. People love their lives along the river and are proud of their lifestyle. In Umaji, the people share this feeling – exemplified by the fact that they now they deliberately use regional dialect, even when talking to outsiders.

Thus, we can say that all three businesses have been effective in the ecological maintenance of human beings as a natural resource. In this sense, the businesses created not only a new value for disregarded materials but also a new value for people.

3 Business innovation for sustainable development:
The cases introduced in this chapter can be called innovative because they involved a new business model, utilizing natural and human resources in new ways.

This kind of innovation cannot serve large markets or make large profits like J-curve, high-tech ventures. Businesses of this kind sell to small niche markets and do not aim at mass production. They do not damage the natural environment and they do not sack employees. Their revenue does not increase dramatically, but is stable and sustainable. In this sense, this kind of innovation may be called "sustainable-type innovation."

The sustainable-type innovation described here is not only important for marginal rural regions but could also have value for large enterprises and their employees all over the world. Looking after the environment is important for everyone, everywhere. And sustainable growth which maintains both employment and resources is an important aim for many countries, particularly advanced countries. The business model represented by these three cases has implications for many enterprises and many countries.

5.9 Conclusion

Several business cases in mountainous rural parts of Japan were described and analyzed. The first case was the Irodori corporation's business selling leaves, the second was the Shimanto Drama Company's business selling wood shavings, and the third case was the Umaji village agriculture union's business selling misshapen yuzu oranges. All three are on Shikoku island.

The three cases have some similarity in their manner of stimulating regional development.

1. In all cases, village people used resources which had no value in a conventional context.
2. Through the success of their businesses, three regional organizations were successful in activating and empowering marginal people in remote areas.
3. This kind of innovation cannot serve large markets or make huge profits like J-curve high-tech ventures; businesses of this sort target small niche markets and are not interested in mass production. At the same time, they do not damage the environment and they do not sack their staff. Their growth of revenue does not increase radically, but is stable and sustainable. Ii is in this sense that these kinds of innovation can be termed "sustainable innovation."

These three cases created not only business resources with new value but also a new value for people. The innovation for sustainable development described here is not only relevant to marginal rural regions but also suggests useful change for large enterprises and their employees all over the world.

Acknowledgments

The author would like to express his thanks to the regional business leaders, Tomoji Yokoishi, Rishou Azechi and Mochifumi Toutani, and many village people for their kind cooperation as interviewees. Thanks are also due to fellow researchers at the Kochi University of Technology for their discussions and useful suggestions on regional issues.

6 Regional community as business platform

6.1 Introduction

In most stagnated rural areas, resource deficiency is a major obstacle for economic development. However, even in such areas, the majority of people possess intangible assets associated with human relationships, resulting from shared history and showing itself in a sense of solidarity, a hometown feeling, a sense of social responsibility, or common ethics and values. Human relationships in themselves are a significant asset for the creation and establishment of a regional business.

In this chapter, four communities of different sizes are compared to clarify the importance of collective in the establishment of a business platform in rural regions and to explore how such platforms might be utilized in concrete business schemes.

The main reason for the comparative analysis is to identify the "common" characteristics of the collective and human networks forming the basis for each business. Thus, four very different business cases have been selected for observation, as described in the following.

Company names and industry fields

Case 1: Taketomi Koutsuu: a transport company (operating tour buses)
Case 2: Iriomote Koutsuu: a transport company with diversification businesses
Case 3: Chikamori-kai: a medical services company
Case 4: Tosa-Senri: a greengrocer's

Scale of business: approximate number of target people and market area

Case 1: 500 people in 10 km^2
Case 2: 6000 people in 300 km^2
Case 3: 150,000 people in 300 km^2
Case 4: 150,000 people in 15,000 km^2

After comparing these four cases in terms of business field, market size and business scale, their common elements will be abstracted.

The aim of the analysis is to isolate the key aspects of the different business models with regard to organization and the management of knowledge. A number of questions guide this analysis.

Business model questions

Question 1: How was the organization and human network established?
Question 2: How is profit made?
Question 3: How do they grow their business?

Since this research is focusing on the collective mission and human network aspects of the cases, the following are also relevant.

Collective mission and human network characteristics

Question 4: What is the nature of the collective mission and how was it established?
Question 5: What are the links between people and how do they communicate?
Question 6: What is the benefit for each member of the human network and organization?

After discussing these four cases, some other cases will be introduced to show the variety of businesses based on community platforms.

6.2 The case of Taketomi island – uniting for survival

Taketomi is a small island in the southern part of Japan, more than 2000 km from Tokyo. The island is three kilometers in diameter, with a periphery of nine kilometers. The total population is around 350. There are thirty-four students at the elementary school and the junior high school. There is only one doctor in the island. Islanders strongly value their traditional culture, as shown by their involvement in the Tanetori Matsuri (harvest festival).

Although the island is very small, it can have around 400,000 tourists a year because its semitropical character is very attractive.

Right after the Second World War there were eighteen tour bus companies on the island. They each operated independently, without taking customer convenience into account. This may have been due to post-war confusion, but in that case the confusion continued for a long time.

Manabu Uema, executive director of Taketomi Koutsuu (Taketomi Transport), a transport/tourism company, came back to the island with his daughter in the 1990s. He said that he was shocked by the chaotic situation he found, because he thought no business could work well in such a manner. He made up his mind to unite those separate companies and rationalize them, to enable them to survive.

Convincing the companies of the advantages of this took five years, but he was eventually successful. The following argument proved decisive: "If you do not unite to realize a rational business system, all your businesses will be lost

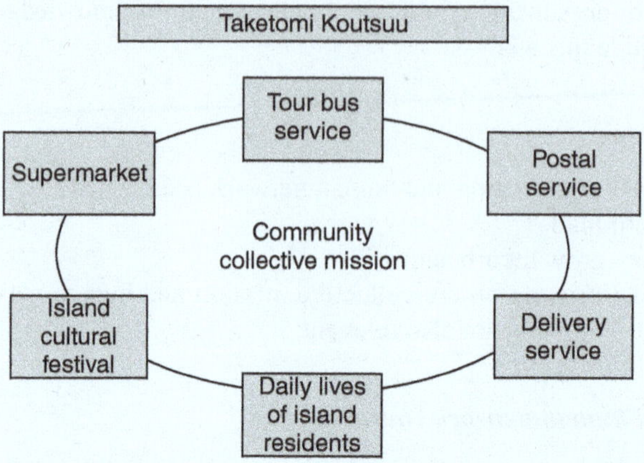

Figure 6.1 Diagram of the Taketomi business and community network.

and your children will never stay on this small island. Don't you care about such a wretched situation?" In line with his proposal, they joined together to form a single tour bus company with a rational schedule, and the collective profit was indeed increased. As a result of these changes, the islanders came to have closer communication with each other and a better system of mutual aid and encouragement

After uniting these enterprises, Mr Uema extended the business to other fields, such as the postal and delivery services. He also plans to launch a supermarket business on the island. All these are businesses which enhance the islanders' daily lives. And they can all be managed by island people, for island people. "Because this is such a tiny island, the people should help each other to survive. That's community life, and community business," he said.

6.3 The case of Iriomote island – diversification businesses for symbiosis

Iriomote is an island close to Taketomi. The island is about 300 km², larger than Taketomi. Its total number of residents is around 2400. Before the Second World War, nobody could live in the island because of malaria mosquitoes. After the war, because the US navy had got rid of the mosquitoes, people could settle from surrounding islands and the Japanese mainland.

The island has beautiful mangroves and a coral shelf and is a national park. Its beauty is widely known and it has some 350,000 visitors a year.

However, in the past, the island was much less well known, and its enterprises consisted only of small dairy units and the growing of sugar cane and pineapples. The cultivation of sugar cane is protected by the government, but pineapples have a different history. The island pineapples used to be bought by the processing factory for twenty-five yen a piece. However, after the first wave of globalization, cheaper pineapples were imported from Vietnam and Taiwan and the island pineapples lost their competitive advantage. Pineapple farmers on the island were at risk of losing their jobs. In response, a man named Masaharu Tamamori and some other islanders decided to go on an island pineapple promotional tour. They visited cities in all parts of the country to advertise the beauty of Iriomote island and its special island products. They have continued these promotional efforts for ten years and successfully established an Iriomote brand. Nowadays, they the island has plenty of tourists and the tourists buy numerous pineapples as souvenirs. These pineapples now sell for 300 to 500 yen per piece. Thus, the price of an island pineapple is currently between ten and twenty times more than before.

Following their success with the pineapples, they have tried to develop other island items, such as Iriomote sake.

The success of the business owes everything to islanders working together, because if they had not joined with each other to participate in the promotional tours, the current level of business could not have been developed. At the same time, the pineapple business group has contributed to island life through extending their enterprises. Mr Tamamori is currently vice president of the Iriomote Koutsuu (Tourism) company, which has diversified into businesses such as a pleasure boat, tourist/commuting buses, a taxi, a hotel, a restaurant, fishing and supermarkets. These many businesses make a real difference to islanders. For example, the two supermarkets are the only stores where islanders can purchase regular items. These supermarkets are not independently profitable, but the company continues to run them because they are so important to islander people. That is the reason why the company has set up so many diversification enterprises. If they manage a range of different enterprises, they can merge the profitability of each one and operate the business as a whole. In concrete terms, the

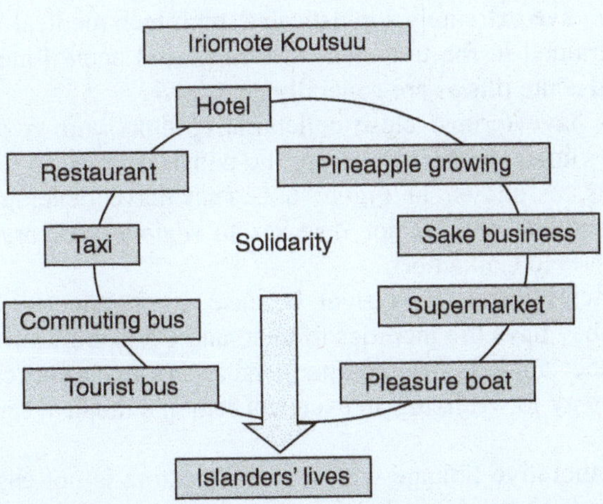

Figure 6.2 Diagram of the Iriomote business and community network.

surplus space in the pleasure boat can be used to transport items for the supermarket, and soap made from recycled oil from the commuting bus can be used in the hotel, and so on. They can unite aspects of the different businesses and help to support the islanders' daily lives. This can be called a symbiotic system or reciprocal supporting system. The mutual dependency of the islanders is also strong simply because they are living on a small island. Although Iriomote is larger than Taketomi, collaboration is just as important for community survival and business success.

6.4 The case of Chikamori Hospital – effective service through community networking

The population of Kochi city, located on Shikoku island, is around 300,000. The Chikamori-kai group has been offering medical services in the center of Kochi for over sixty years. They have around 1200 employees (1500 including outsourced labor), and about 650 inpatients and 650 outpatients a day, amounting to more than 10,000 patients a year (mostly from Kochi prefecture.)

From the viewpoint of business, the remarkable feature of this medical organization is its strong financial status. The total revenue in 2006 was about 13.3 billion yen and the profit of the same year was about 750 million yen (5.7 percent of revenue). The revenue was more than three times that of 1984. In addition, over those two decades, the profit was almost doubled, the number of doctors increased five-fold, the number of nurses ten-fold, and the number of employees and number of patients both trebled.

One reason for this financial success is the unit price of their hospital service. For example, in Chikamori hospital, one of their four group hospitals, the average charge is about 70,000 yen per person per day, which is the top price in Japan. The question is then how they can impose such a high hospital charge. To answer this question, there are two keys.

One reason is that they have extremely sophisticated, high-tech medical facilities and doctors highly trained in the treatment of critical and acute illnesses. Treatments for critical and acute illness are generally expensive.

Another factor is they have formed close collaborative links with regional doctors and small private clinics in order to secure the patients for those highly priced medical treatments, as shown in Figure 6.3. They have developed a system which transfers patients with minor diseases to regional doctors and patients with serious diseases to Chikamori.

Both sides benefit financially from this system, because regional doctors have a proper flow of patients they have the facilities to treat, and Chikamori-kai is in a position to confidently specialize. It is a good partnership and also a successful organized positioning strategy for realizing an excellent regional medical service for rural residents.

This kind of tight collaborative linkage with regional doctors is not easy to build up because there needs to be close, daily communication and the maintenance of face-to-face relationships. It would be almost impossible in a large

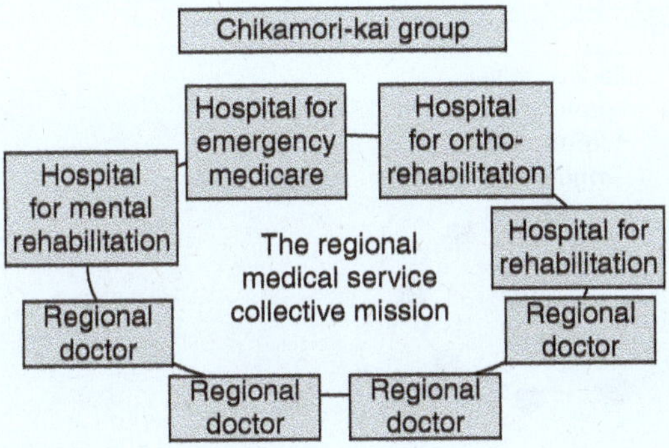

Figure 6.3 Diagram of the Chikamori business and community network.

metropolitan city. In middle-sized Kochi, Chikamori-kai has put effort into forming close relationship with doctors in the region, inviting them to free training lectures on up-to-date medical technologies, facilitating the exchange of information about patients and treatment facilities, and so on. These human network links are the very basis of their profitable business model.

6.5 The case of Tosa-Senri – a grocery with information and human networks

Tosa-Senri is a business selling vegetables and other food items produced in Kochi prefecture. Its employees number only two, with about ten temporary staff members. Its customers are from Senri New Town, a large residential area in north Osaka, 12 km from the center, built around 1960. The zone has department stores, shopping malls, libraries, primary schools, junior high schools, high schools, numerous offices, and so on. Its total area is about 15,000 m^2 and the number of residents once reached 130,000. Although the shop itself was rather small, it served a large consumer zone, including Senri New Town, Osaka and the wider area of Kochi prefecture.

The Tosa-Senri business policy was to deal only in high-quality, specialist vegetables and food items, coming, as far as possible, from within the prefecture, because the mission from the start of the enterprise was to support local producers.

Usually, speciality stores of this kind do not make much money and have a poor financial status. However, Tosa-Senri has recorded outstandingly good financial returns, with the tiny staff team generating annual sales of over 100 million yen. The main reason for their success is their communication style. They learn as much as possible about the products – their unique characteristics and how to cook them – by visiting the farmers/producers, and then pass this on to their shop customers in the form of readily accessible information sheets. They also try to talk to their customers about the products in order to provide

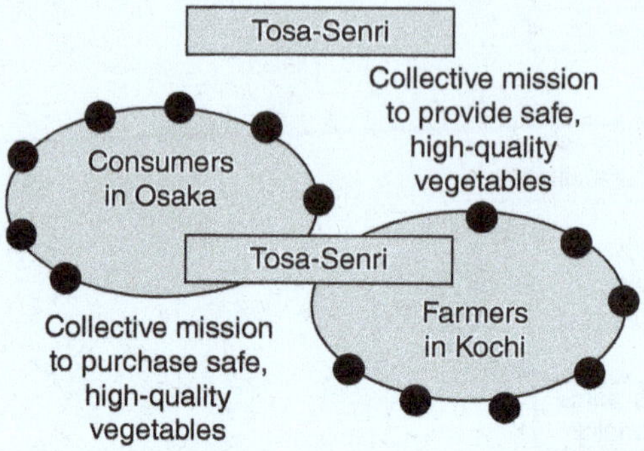

Figure 6.4 Diagram of the Tosa-Senri.business and community network.

producers with useful feedback. Many customers find this style of business satisfactory. Tosa-Senri has established strong connections with numerous farmers in Kochi and also with many consumers in Osaka. That is, it has built close links between producers and consumers and this has led directly to unusually high sales figures. This linkage was based on shared standards, such as an appreciation of high-quality, safe foods, a moral/ethical desire to sell consumers only products of this sort, and a high value attached to things natural associated with what might be called the "slow life."

A schematic illustration of the Tosa-Senri business model and the collective mission and human network used in the business are shown in Figure 6.4.

6.6 Comparative analysis of the four cases

By observing these four cases, we can see that human networks and collaborative activity was indispensable for all of them. On a small and isolated island like Taketomi, people would not have achieved anything without mutual aid. The situation is similar on Iriomote island, where collaboration and reciprocal support systems based on solidarity proved equally essential for survival.

Similarly, with a medium-scale regional business like Chikamori-kai, network collaboration and positioning in the network structure was crucial to the success of their business model. Even with Tosa-Senri, a retail business in a large city, it is the close communication within the network of consumers and producers that forms the basis of its success. The connection between people in a retail business of this kind comprises shared views in relation to product quality and certain life values.

With reference to the questions first posed in section 6.2, it becomes clear that a collective mission and human network played a significant role in all their business models.

The findings may be summarized as follows.

1 Members of the business organization and its associated networks exchange explicit knowledge and also share their tacit knowledge of business or technology.
2 To form such human networks, close communication and frequent face-to-face contact are important.
3 A strong sense of collective mission is also necessary for strong human networks, particularly with long-term business schemes.
4 With smaller-scale business areas, the sense of solidarity resulting from daily community life or strong hometown affection can itself form the basis of a collective mission.
5 With larger-scale business areas, a collective mission requires a sense of social responsibility and shared moral and ethical values, in addition to short-term common interests.
6 Human networks, built on collective missions, make up the business platforms which are the basis of these business models.

This is shown schematically in Figures 6.5 and 6.6.

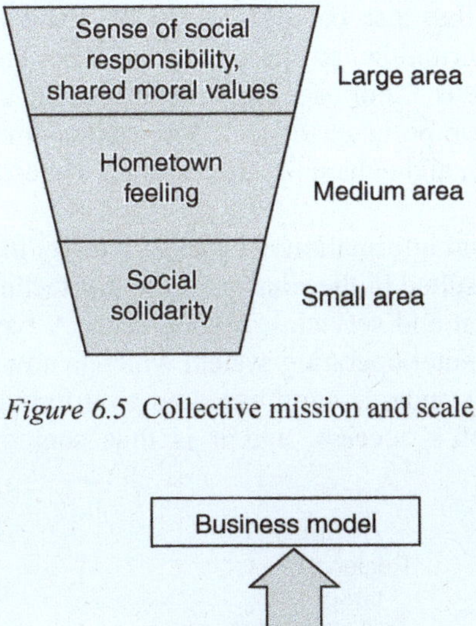

Figure 6.5 Collective mission and scale of community (market) area.

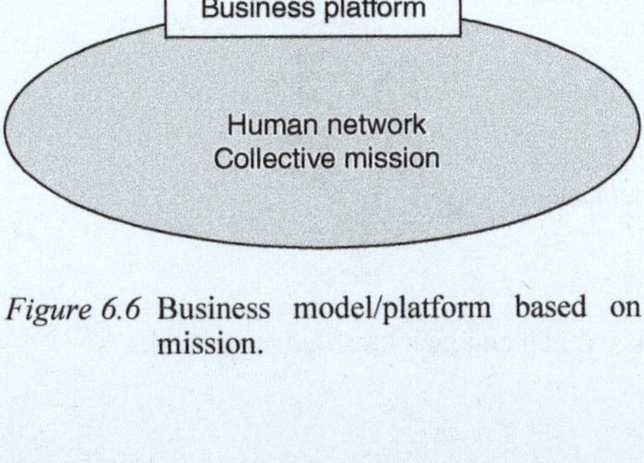

Figure 6.6 Business model/platform based on human network and collective mission.

Let us now consider the link between knowledge management and human relations.

As discussed in Chapter 2, knowledge is now central to societal and business development. Many people call this the era of the "Knowledge-based Society." The nature of "knowledge" in this context was explored by numerous researchers in the 1990s. Badaracco (1991) and Nonaka and Takeuchi (1995) have identified two kinds of knowledge: one is "explicit knowledge" and the other is "tacit knowledge." Explicit knowledge is portable because it is expressed as documentation or some other tangible information form outside of human beings; in contrast, tacit knowledge is not portable because it is embedded inside of human beings as an intangible asset. Innovation is created by the circulation of both explicit and tacit knowledge, and, as Nonaka and Takeuchi explained, the sharing of tacit knowledge is as significant for the induction of innovation as the sharing of explicit knowledge via the information network.

Regarding the competence of enterprises in the present world, Porter (1990) argued that forming regional industrial clusters, like the information technology industry cluster in Silicon Valley, can lead to significant competitive advantage. Porter pointed out the important role of knowledge (technological expertise, business know-how, new ideas, and so on) in the formation of such clusters, and his concept of industrial clustering can thus also be characterized as knowledge linkage among regional people or opportunities to share tacit business knowledge, as schematically shown in Figure 6.7. Porter's thesis regarding the competence of industries is related to the importance of tacit knowledge linkage among people in encouraging innovation and enhancing the strength of business enterprises.

This is also the era of globalization and information networks. In many industries, the rapid growth of markets has resulted in the standardization of technologies/goods for low-cost mass production and servicing convenience. A typical example is the Microsoft Windows computer operating system which is now virtually standard all over the world. This standardization based on an information network became the basis of Microsoft's success, and it is thus sometimes

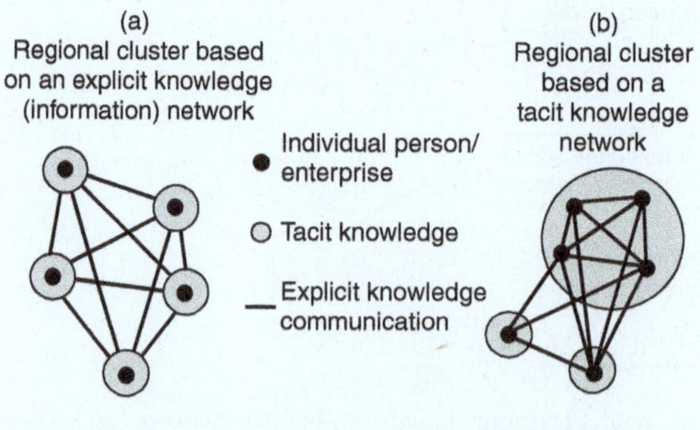

Figure 6.7 Regional clusters as explicit and tacit knowledge networks.

termed their business platform. Gawer and Cusumano (2002) referred in detail to the characteristics of this phenomenon, and emphasized the importance of leadership in the development of business platforms which enable survival in current critical market conditions.

Standardization as a business platform based on an information network is basically a matter of explicit knowledge. The remaining question is, therefore, "what is a business platform based on tacit knowledge?" because tacit knowledge is the other important element in the search for innovation and competitiveness.

This chapter discusses the role of local people's collective mission in relation to "tacit knowledge networks" for business innovation, looking at business platforms based on tacit knowledge or human networks, with particular respect to issues of regional development.

For this purpose, four illustrative cases in Japan were examined in terms of how human networks and collective missions can contribute to business success. Each case belongs to a different business category and has a different scale of business, market and organization. Through comparing these four cases and analyzing their similarities and differences, the common characteristics of business architecture and the role of human networks and collective missions can be discussed.

The human network as discussed in this chapter is schematically drawn in Figure 6.8. If the business area is small, the network is almost same as the regional cluster shown in Figure 6.7 (b). If the business area is large, as with Tosa-Senri, the network extends beyond the border of the locality, as shown as (c) in Figure 6.8, contrasting with (b). We may call this a clustering network, after the regional cluster.

In order to form clustering human networks sharing tacit knowledge, people need some kind of collective mission to unite them. Thus, collective missions can be a basis not only of human networks but also knowledge networks, acting as a business platform for innovation.

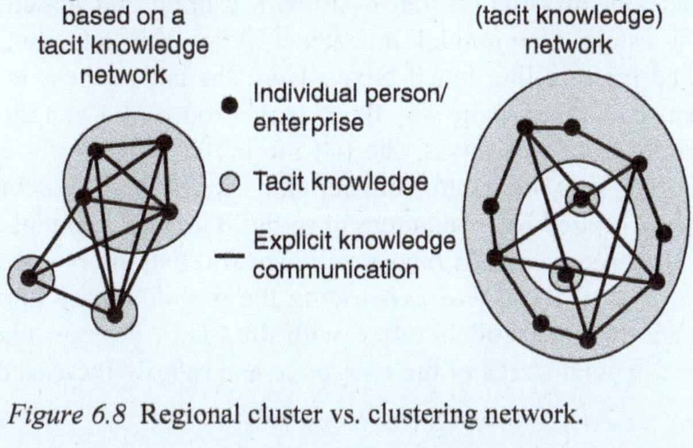

Figure 6.8 Regional cluster vs. clustering network.

The clustering network represents, for contemporary business, an alternative kind of business platform to the well-known platform based on information networks illustrated in Figure 6.7 (a).

Figure 6.8 indicates that knowledge networks which combine the sharing of tacit knowledge and the sharing of explicit knowledge make a strong platform for business. Information networks can be easily enlarged by communication technology, for example the internet. By contrast, tacit knowledge networks cannot be easily enlarged, because of the physical limitations of networking; nevertheless, they can sometimes form a very effective business platform for a particular business model. The cases studied in this chapter could not have been established without a business platform of this sort.

6.7 The case of Yumenomachi Souzouiinkai – an ICT enterprise with a social mission

The next case offers some insight into the relationship between ICT networking and human networking,

The headquarters of the enterprise called Yumenomachi Souzouiinkai (which translates as "The Committee for Creating the City of Dreams") is located in Osaka, the biggest city in West Japan. Not only the name of the enterprise, but also its characteristics are very unusual. In 2008, its capitalization was about one billion yen and annual sales were some 800 million yen (with a profit ratio of around 30 percent). There were forty-seven employees. The enterprise was established in 1999 and they launched their internet portal site, called Demaekan, in 2000. Demaekan is a portal site for people seeking food delivery services. If they enter the site, they can input their home address, and then quickly and easily learn which restaurants can deliver which dishes according to what time schedule and at what price.

The enterprise rapidly grew after the appointment of a charismatic CEO called Toshie Nakamura. Ms Nakamura has been a remarkable businessperson since she was a student, when she established a wake-up call service for fellow students. After graduating from university, she joined a real estate enterprise and had considerable sales success by adopting a value-added marketing strategy. That is, she researched the information that customers wanted and added this when selling the real estate commercial magazine. After this success, she switched to another enterprise selling lunch-boxes. Here she had success in significantly reducing costs by changing the way flyers were produced. Even though she was promoted rapidly in this business, she left the job in order to focus on her children. In 2001, the Yumenomachi Souzouiinkai enterprise had debts of 300 million yen, and they invited Ms Nakamura to re-build its management. She very quickly effected the organization's recovery by several extremely successful business strategies. One of these was penetrating the mobile phone internet service industry, and another was collaborating with the major internet player, Yahoo. She rebuilt the financial status of the enterprise and rapidly increased the value of its stock.

In addition to running the Demaekan site, they launched a new portal service called Kaketsukekan, which means "delivery service for everything." This included computer and machinery repair, cleaning, chauffering, recycling, removals, window replacement, the duplication of keys and many other service areas.

The enterprise's organization can be called an autonomous distributed system. The structure of the organization is flat and every employee can access management information, including financial information, through the internet. The autonomy, identity and independence of each employee is respected as a top priority. The average age of employees is thirty-two, and 40 percent of managers are female.

The CEO, Ms Nakamura, spent 40 percent of her time educating employees and encouraging them to launch their own businesses separately from Yumenomachi Souzouiinkai. Basically, she respected the independence of each employee and aimed to see them disperse to run their own start-ups. She said that the mission of the enterprise was to contribute to society and develop independent people.

The characteristics of this enterprise are very unusual and interesting. In a sense, it provides a portal site system and organization as a business platform for each employee, and hopes each one can, in time, autonomously establish their own business on the platform. In this case, the enterprise plays the role of community in supporting people establish new enterprises.

6.8 The case of Wanowakai – a regional non-profit organization

In a small, resource-poor region, people have to work together at the level of their daily lives. In such instances, community plays a pivotal role in the support of each individual.

Wanowakai, which means "circle of linkage," is a non-profit organization (NPO) established in 2005 in a village called Hidaka. Its activities cover childcare, care of the elderly, support for handicapped persons, by collaborating public office and agriculture union. Only a few individuals initiated the project, but its membership grew to sixty in a couple of years. The NPO mission is "(1) To develop community businesses for solving our day-to-day problems ourselves. (2) To provide job opportunities for local people. (3) To motivate and support everyone in the community, including senior citizens and the handicapped." The methodology behind its activities is collaboration, mutual aid and the exchange of roles to provide services flexibly. That is, if a certain housewife cannot care for her child on a certain day, another person will provide that childcare service. And in exchange, the housewife will, for instance, help in the café restaurant or with the care of an elderly person. Wanowakai is active across numerous areas:

1 Advertizing section: community newspaper, community website;
2 Community support: health center, day care service, lunch delivery service, tomato-growing operation;

3 Business: café restaurant, processed food manufacture, marketing and product planning;
4 Childcare: small private school, kids' club;
5 Training: assistance with the search for work, preparation for work, group living;
6 Education: care services training, management and project management training, development of performance artists;
7 Supporting local lives: daily homecare services (bathing, toileting, help with meals, etc.).

All members can join in any of the activities which offer support, instead of only receiving support from others. The level of participation is flexible, tailored to each member's availability. One member might take part in activities once a week and another every day. A representative of the NPO said: "It's not good that some people always help others, and others are always being helped by somebody. Each person should offer support to someone else, even if he/she is a handicapped person. Nobody is special but all are normal in this system."

To look at one area, the NPO established a processing business associated with tomato production. In Hidaka there were more than ten tomato farms, producing eight tons of misshapen tomatoes unfit for the market. The NPO purchased around three tons of these tomatoes and turned them into jams and sauces. And they set this up so that handicapped persons could take part. As a result, the project turned misshapen tomatoes into marketable commodities and at the same time provided a place of work for handicapped persons.

This is a typical example of people collaborating for mutual benefit at the level of daily life within a regional community. The unity and solidarity of community acts as a platform for their business and personal lives.

6.9 The case of Obuse city – an autonomous community with a common mission

Respect for community and community culture rather than economic development can sometimes be the goal for regional people.

Obuse is a small old town with a population of around 10,000 in a mountain area in Nagano prefecture. The town is famous for its traditional cake made from chestnuts, and their sake is another regional product.

The people so value their town that they undertook its renovation themselves. Each household agreed to do up their property in the traditional style, using traditional materials. Even the pavements of the town were refurbished, with chestnut blocks arranged in beautiful patterns. People are proud of the appearance of their town and the culture of the region; even a pupil at the elementary school expressed this feeling of pride.

An American woman from Pennsylvania called Sarah Marie Cummings, became manager of the town's traditional sake brewing enterprise and she has planned and executed many interesting events for regional development. Once a month she organizes a special lecture, inviting guest speakers such as architects, artists, musicians, novelists or academics, and over 3000 people attend from all over the country or even from abroad. After the lecture, all the visitors are invited to a party held in the traditional chestnut cake store. The lectures are then published as magazines.

The town runs many other events, including half-marathons, art exhibitions and concerts. As a result, there are over one million visitors to the town. But the townspeople said that the aim of their activities was not economic development but the popularization of their culture. They can be said to have open minds, as indicated by their building a chest hospital in the Meiji period, over a hundred years ago. At that time, chest disease was thought to be dangerously infectious and, naturally, no one was keen to have such a hospital in their area. However, the people of Obuse agreed to the hospital because of their generosity and humanism. They are proud of having such a history.

Similarly to Hidaka city, the people of the region have a strong solidarity and share common ideals; the establishment of their businesses – processed foods, chestnut cake-making, sake brewing, and so on – are based on these attitudes.

Again, in this town, regional community plays the part of business platform.

6.10 Conclusion

In the first part of this chapter, four kinds of enterprise (business case), Taketomi Koutsuu, Iriomote Koutsuu, Chilamori-kai and Tosa-Senri, were described and analyzed.

As a result of the analysis, we conclude that, in a knowledge-based society, the importance of human network as business platform is growing. Also, collective mission is a key element in the formation of human networks, and thus hometown feelings, feelings of solidarity and shared values and moral standards within a community are intangible assets forming the basis of regional business. Whether it is a large enterprise or a small or medium enterprise, some kind of collective mission and human network would seem to be required to establish the business platform.

The findings of this study are summarized as follows.

1 Human networks play a significant role in business models for regional development.
2 In such human networks, people exchange explicit knowledge, and they also share tacit knowledge relating to business or technology through frequent contact and/or face-to-face communication.
3 To form a human network of this sort, there needs to be a strong sense of collective mission for the community living in the business area. This is particularly necessary with long-term business schemes.

These implications have relevance not only for regional development but also for many contemporary enterprises wishing to survive in the present competitive global market. Regardless of the scale or field of business, there are similarities regarding effective business strategies in our knowledge-based society.

In the latter part of this chapter, three other cases were introduced and analyzed. These cases indicated that some communities act as business platforms, with each member of the community playing an active business part. In such communities, every person is independent and autonomous, while respecting all other community members and the community culture.

To confirm the universality of these implications, additional business cases should be researched. These case study analyses should also add detail to the characteristics of clustering human networks.

Acknowledgments

The author would like to express his sincere appreciation to the many businesspersons who enabled the collection of information about the companies examined here, including Teruko Kedashiro, Sakiko Kedashiro, Yasushi Yagi, Takayuki Iriomote, Manabu Uema, Masamichi Tamamori, Masaharu Tamamori, Noboru Kawazoe, Mariko Tomita, Kouji Usui, Chharu Yasuoka, Etsuko Seki, Tsuguo Ichimura, Sarah Marie Cummings and many others.

7 Sustainable development via community design

7.1 Introduction

In the regions, many private businesses are tightly connected to their local communities. One reason is that people in the regions cannot live without help from other community members. For disaster prevention, keeping safe, maintaining the infrastructure and public services, carrying out fishing and farming, and so on, regional people need to support each other across many scenarios. Particularly in resource-poor rural regions experiencing aging and depopulation, people must work together in order to survive. In this sense, establishing a business in a rural region cannot be separated from considerations of the design of regional community and the development of a whole community economy.

This chapter discusses different kinds of community redesign, looking at two depopulated regions, one a central metropolitan area and the other a remote mountain area, where there have been programs for development through art. As mentioned in Chapter 4, art can be a very accessible and powerful tool for vitalizing resource-poor regions. In those cases, the economic effect was not the main issue. In the cases in this chapter, the use of art as a tool for regional development did have economic impact and, moreover, the regions planned to restructure their industries for more sustainable community development.

What was important was that the regional leaders, as social entrepreneurs, had a vision of renovating their regional communities and industrial structure for sustainable development. It was from this perspective that they took action. The detailed strategies and practices of their programs are illustrated in the following sections.

7.2 The case of the Bakuro CET scheme – renovation of a depopulated district

7.2.1 Overview of the CET movement

Many regions are facing a crisis of depopulation and possible extinction not only remote areas but also some stagnated areas in cities.

Bakuro district, in Tokyo, was just such a stagnated area. In the past, the district had a prosperous fashion industry and there were numerous businesses associated with the textile and clothing trade. However, the fashion industry in Japan suffered from competition with emerging countries and the district became depressed. There were many unoccupied houses and warehouses.

Kazushige Toriyama is a long-term resident of the district and the second-generation owner of a business making towels. He is an active individual with a strong and lasting desire to contribute to the community. The CET movement is greatly indebted to his efforts.

The Central East of Tokyo (CET) movement was initiated by some individuals who were involved in another movement called Tokyo Designers' Block (TDB), which aimed to stimulate regional development through art and design. TDB was mainly active in the Aoyama area, the center of Tokyo. CET was named after TDB to suggest the similarity of its purpose.

TDB put on exhibitions for artists and designers in Aoyama shops and coffee houses, but CET planned to hold exhibitions in empty houses and warehouses.

Kazushige Toriyama and Yoshitugu Shimizu – an architect involved in city planning – met at a meeting of the committee preparing for the four hundredth anniversary of the foundation of Edo (Tokyo). Mr Shimizu introduced the movement of TDB to Mr Toriyama, and this triggered the establishment of CET.

CET was organized by a group of around fifty people. Mr Toriyama was responsible for selecting vacant house/shop/warehouse spaces for exhibitions and negotiating as necessary with the owners and any public officials, because he had strong connections with local people. Everything was done by via Mr Toriyama's personal links and communication channels. In this way, his role in the project was critical.

Meanwhile, the selection of artists and designers, totalling over 200, was done by professional producers, and eventually numerous artists and designers from Shanghai, New York, London and other major centers areas joined in the project.

For the participating artists, it was an opportunity to exhibit their artworks to a large audience, which made the project very attractive to them.

The working expenditure for the project was funded by the space charge paid by artists, advertisement fees, and donations. Funding money was between one million and ten million yen (1000 and 10,000 US dollars) depending on the year.

The project was also of benefit to many students of art, architecture and media, because if they joined the project as volunteers they could talk directly with well-known artists. Over 200 volunteers were recruited as interns through the internet.

The event has been held over ten days every October each year since 2003. In the third year, they had over eight million visitors. The event has also been enlarged gradually. In addition to art exhibitions, concerts and street parties now take place. At the parties, young people and local women serve food to the visitors and enjoy the occasion with them.

At the beginning, local people were not interested in art or art events, but as time went on, they started to see the value of a scheme which makes their area appeal to outsiders. Television programs about of some of the events have caused the district to be even more widely known.

A lot of younger people began to visit the district, not only during the exhibition period, and this has brought in contemporary galleries and restaurants. Nowadays, there are over thirty galleries, numerous coffee shops and restaurants and a great variety of stores. This has attracted younger people to move to the area and the rental value of property has increased.

This is an account of the successful revitalization and economic development of an area through art.

7.2.2 The contribution of a social entrepreneur and his ideas on renovating a region

As already mentioned, Mr Toriyama was extremely important to the success of CET. We might call him a social entrepreneur.

In general, proposals to utilize vacant shops in a stagnated shopping arcade in the regions as galleries for development projects are unsuccessful because the shop owners do not like to rent their shops to anyone else. This has been a barrier for regional development projects in many places. However, in this case, Mr Toriyama had become popular in the area due to his involvement in local festivals and other regional activities, and his overtures to shop owners were received more positively. This was key to the success of the project.

In 2005, when the event was clearly launched, Mr Toriyama stood down as chair of the project committee to focus more on preparing young people to continue the movement.

During the interview he talked about the idea of designing regional community. He mentioned the fact that, 400 years ago, Bakuro district was a place of hotels for travellers. It was named Bakuro, meaning horse eating, because of the feeding of travellers' horses during the Edo era.

At that time, the town followed a policy of what could be called ecological circulation. That is, the busiest shops in the town were located in the main street and the start-ups began their business in the back streets where the rents were low. If the start-ups were successful, they moved to the main street and new start-ups took their place. This kind of business circulation activated the town like a living thing. Mr Toriyama dreamt of reviving this circulation to vitalize the town and bring about sustainable development. For bringing about such changes in the community, an art project proved very effective.

It was fortunate for Bakuro that such an enthusiastic social entrepreneur was living in the district. The involvement of committed social entrepreneurs like him with a strong feeling of hometown have been key to the success of regional development through art in many instances.

To summarize, this project in Bakuro was started by the personal intention and passion of Mr Toriyama, and has continued due to a great deal of collaborative input by local people.

It has resulted in many new coffee shops, restaurants, fashion boutiques, contemporary galleries and jewellery shops in the town. These shops have attracted the younger generation and the number of young people moving to the area is growing. The rents of shops and apartments in the district have gone up as a result, and thus the project has contributed to the district's economic development.

7.3 The case of the Kamiyama artist-in-residence scheme – redesigning rural community

7.3.1 Overview of the artist-in-residence movement

The city of Kamiyama in Nanishigun, Tokushima prefecture, is located in a remote mountain area forty minutes by car from Tokushima. There are hot springs in the city and tourism is one of its main industries.

Shinya Ominami was born in Kamiyama and entered Nihon University to learn civil engineering before succeeding to his father's construction business. He also travelled to the US as an exchange graduate school student and spent two years there.

After graduating from graduate school, he came back to Kamiyama and was involved in regional development as a youth member of the Chamber of Commerce and Industry.

For the first ten years he was engaged in events organized according to customary regional development methodology. He was passionate about these various projects but they were not successful and he became discouraged.

Once he heard that there was an old doll gifted from someone in the US to Shinryou Elementary School. He visited the school, from which he had graduated twenty years previously, because he was very interested in the story of the doll, and gathered as much information as possible.

In 1927, 12,739 dolls named Alice with blue eyes were gifted from the US to Japan, and 152 of them were transferred to Kochi as part of the cultural exchange.

Unfortunately, most of the dolls were destroyed or lost because they had been made in what became the enemy country. However, it was believed that some 300 still existed, one of them being the doll in the Shinryou school. With the doll was a document described as doll's passport, with the name of the town where the doll was made. The doll in Kamiyama came from Wilkinsberg in Pennsylvania, US. Mr Ominami was extremely interested in this doll and wanted to look for the person who had gifted the doll sixty-four years before. With help from Wilkinsberg he finally traced the person but discovered that, regrettably, he had already died.

Despite this, the search helped to develop a relationship between the two cities and around thirty people, including Mr Ominami, later visited Wilkinsberg. They suggested a new exchange of dolls and in 1992, established the International Exchange Association in Kamiyama, which continued various sorts of exchange activities for a while.

These activities prompted a certain amount of regional development in Kamiyama, but gradually people became bored by its limited remit.

In 1997, Tokushima prefecture proposed setting up a village of international culture. Mr Ominami and his colleagues thought this could be an excellent opportunity to enhance existing development activities. However, they recognized that there was a tendency, with many publicly funded projects, for people to depend too much on the public service input and fail to continue the project when this support came to an end. So Mr Ominami and the others decided to take the initiative and support the scheme independently.

The two pillars of the project were "Environment" and "Art." They made reference to a US "adopt' scheme for activities related to the environment and drew on an existing Japanese artist residence program for the art activities. The art residence program had already been tried on Awaji island and in the city of Tosa in Kochi.

The adopt scheme was initiated in Texas in 1985. Called Adopt-a-Highway, it involved individual or group sponsorship of the cleaning of sections of highway, with the regional office running a bulletin board to show who donated the money.

The basic idea was to have a public welfare service supported by citizens rather than the local authority. Mr Ominami had seen this scheme in action during his staying in the US and was motivated to try and make it work in Japan.

The resident artist scheme was a plan to invite three artists from outside the region, including from abroad, and fund them to stay in the city for two months to make an artwork. By limiting the number of artists to three, the cost was relatively low and the local authority would be able to support the project for the first few years. It was an achievable idea.

It is often said that exchange with the outside world is essential for regional development. In this case, Mr Ominami was the window to the outside world, bringing in fresh ideas. His experience in the US and his English language capability were valuable tools.

In 2004, Mr Ominami founded an NPO, Green Valley, to advance the development movement. This worked with Tokushima prefecture to set up an artist-in-residence scheme in Kamiyama. They did not fix the categories of art and aimed to recruit three artists, helped by the curator of the Tokushima Prefectural Museum. In the first year of the project, four artists applied. One aspect of the selection criteria was affinity with the region, the ability to relate to the natural environment of Kamiyama and establish good relationships with local people. The other was the quality of the artist's work, mainly judged by the curator.

In the second year of the project, there were seven applicants, and gradually the criteria of artist selection became a major issue. In the end, because the main purpose of the project was regional development, affinity with the region was given the most weight in the selection process.

The number of applicants can now be as many as ninety and the selection procedure has become more complex. In the first stage, the committee, made up of local people, make up a shortlist of thirty artists, taking into account existing artwork and affinity with the region. In the second stage, they discuss the selection with teachers from art schools and museum curators, and select the final three. Exactly which experts they invite is significant. They look for those who can understand the purpose of the scheme and the character of the region. Nowadays the selection system operates smoothly and the choices of local people are very much in accord with those of the professors.

The project is now in its thirteenth year and its rules have changed a little. In the beginning, the artists were asked to continue to maintain their artworks even after their departure. This maintenance is now waived. Regional people have become familiar with contemporary art through the selection process. Some people have helped artists with their work, thrown a party for them and even discussed their artworks with them. Some artists have revisited the region to make artwork independently and formed close links with local people.

7.3.2 The contribution of a social entrepreneur and his ideas on renovating a region

In this case too, a social entrepreneur played an important role in regional development. Mr Ominami was just the right person to open up the region to the outside world. His experience of living in a foreign country, his foreign language ability and his knowledge of art and architecture were all key to the success of the various Kamiyama projects.

Of course, the basic liveliness of regional people and the collaboration between Mr Ominami and regional staff are also essential elements.

Regarding the impact of the scheme, Mr Ominami in summary said that the first ten years were a period of social and emotional development. During this period, local people were very much stimulated by art events and through exchanges with people from outside the area.

He said the next ten years were characterized by economic development. The number of young people moving to the city from other parts of Japan and becoming involved in craft, media and other kinds of art enterprise has increased. The activity of these people will be the basis of new industries in the city.

Mr Ominami expects that, in the next ten years, the city itself will change. He advocates "creatively designing depopulated regional community" as a new methodology for regional development. He pointed out that it has become difficult to vitalize regions or regional communities within the conventional industrial framework. "To change the framework of industries is essential for the survival of the region," he said in the interview. "An important thing for the region is that newcomers can bring new businesses to the region and we can reconstruct the framework of industries in the region by the power of the newcomers. We must draw newcomers with promising businesses into the region," he said, in explaining his development strategy.

A good example is a project by Tokyo Art University. It sent around 200 students to help in renovating an old vacant house in the city. The project was supported financially by the local authority, which gave it a subsidy of two million yen. The total budget for the renovation was three and a half million yen. The house was renovated as a modern office and was rented by an internet shopping business. The enterprise utilized the office for making commercial movies and as an apartment for the makers of movies. Before renovation the owner thought that the house would be rented for 5000 yen per month, but after renovation the house was rented for 30,000 yen per month. The initial loan for renovating the house has been repaid.

This project triggered an initiative by the Green Valley NPO, chaired by Mr Ominami, to promote immigration to the region on behalf of the local authority. More precisely, the local authority established a regional immigration centre and, in October 2007, entrusted the running of the service to the NPO in. The NPO studied house vacancies in the city, and launched an internet site to recruit tenants for vacant houses in 2008. They got many more applicants than they expected and realized they had a long-term strategy for regional immigration to the city.

Their strategy is as follows: Attract immigrant people with occupations useful for the future of the city and reconstruct the industrial framework of the city, using the power of the immigrants to realize the city's sustainable development. Through this restructuring of the industries, they aim to increase the number of young people staying in the city.

The basic concept of developing the region and designing regional community is based on the insight gained from analyzing the reasons for depopulation.

Mr Ominami explained the mechanism of economic stagnation and the depopulation of the city as follows: There used to be a lively shopping arcade, including a theatre, named the Yorii Shopping Arcade. However, the arcade has stagnated like those in many other regional cities. The main reason for its stagnation is that large modern shops based on high-volume sales have taken their customers from them, just as elsewhere. Mr Ominami pointed out that if the local shopping arcade had some core competence, it could survive. In order to create this additional value and core competence, they needed craftpersons with unique skills. That is why they endeavour to attract skilled immigrant craftpersons.

An example here is the story of a craft baker named Mitsunori Kamimoto, recently immigrated to the city. He makes delicious bread using a genuine stone oven and this bread got so popular it even attracted customers from outside the city. In the end, half the customers of the bread shop came from outside the area. "Selling original items made by craftspeople is an essential strategy to develop a core competence for the local shopping arcade and give it a competitive advantage over the mass-sale shops," Mr Ominami pointed out. "And utilizing the internet is another key way for regional shops to enlarge their market, even in a regional city with low consumption levels," he added.

Mr Ominami began his contribution to the region by planning and executing art events, like the artist-in-residence scheme. But now he has become a strategic planner or a designer of regional community. His main strategy is attracting immigrant artists/craftpersons with unique skills and reconstructing regional industries. Even in a small city, by selling value-added items through both real shops and the internet, a sustainable regional community can be developed. He said, "We cannot stop the flow of depopulation in rural areas, but at least we can make it, through design, 'creative depopulation'."

Following this strategy, they have attracted thirty-six immigrants in two and a half years. The average age of these immigrants is under thirty and they include some from outside Japan.

7.4 Analysis and discussion

7.4.1 Three basic conditions for the development of resource-poor regions

Two cases of economic regional development were introduced in this chapter. The first case involved a metropolitan area of Tokyo and the second a remote mountain area in Tokushima prefecture, but both cases were economically stagnated and depopulated regions suffering from severe competition in the newly global marketplace. In that sense, both cases are typical of struggling resource-poor regions all over the world.

Both cases lacked business resources in the form of tangible assets such as advanced technologies, natural resources or cultural heritage. They were powerless to establish new business by themselves.

In both cases, the trigger for development was an art event, because not a lot of money is needed to initiate art events and they can attract people from outside. For this reason, art events are a very useful tool for the development of resource-poor regions.

However, although art events were a vital starting point, the following conditions were necessary for successful development:

1 Existence of a social entrepreneur with a specific strategy
2 Accumulation of social capital as a basis for development
3 Assistance by outside agency or local authority

Each condition will be detailed in turn.

7.4.2 Existence of a social entrepreneur with a specific strategy

Both cases had an enthusiastic social entrepreneur as a leader of development. The existence of such a person is a minimum condition for regional development, because the task is extremely challenging and there are many obstacles: strong leadership is needed to overcome barriers.

To lead the movement to success, a social entrepreneur should have certain characteristics. In the following section the basic conditions for and characteristics of the successful social entrepreneur are discussed.

a Capability of exchange with the outside world

Art is a convenient tool for the development of regions without business resources; however, who can bring art to regions and who can organize art events aimed at vitalizing regions are the important questions. The involvement of a number of artists, not just one, is necessary, so there is a need for someone able of call on artists from the outside world.

A social entrepreneur should be capable of communicating with the outside world and bringing artists in to the region. In both our cases, a social entrepreneur as regional leader acted as a window to the outside world for this purpose.

Mr Toriyama in Bakurocho was not an artist himself but he had many artist friends when he was young, as well as close connections with many business persons outside the region. The meeting of Mr Toriyama and members of the TDB was a crucial trigger for the setting up of CET. Because he had many artist friends and was familiar with the daily lives of artists, he was at home in the CET movement and became a conduit between artists and local people. If he had not negotiated with the owners of buildings and shops to provide space for exhibitions, the CET program could not have been realized.

Mr Ominami in Kamiyama was also familiar with art, having majored in architecture at university. He was also very capable of communicating with foreigners and introducing foreign culture or ideas to the region as a result of staying in the US when he was at graduate school. The "adopt" and "artist-in-residence" programs were the main triggers for the development of Kamiyama, and those projects were both suggested by Mr Ominami. He was the very person for exchanges with the outside world.

A successful social entrepreneur should have the capability of exchange with the outside world and this is observed not only in the two cases introduced here but also in many other cases of regional development.

b Affinity with the regional community

A successful social entrepreneur should have strong links not only with the outside world but also with the local community. This is another important factor for the success of regional development movements.

Mr Toriyama was very much a local man, inheriting his father's business, a towel manufacturing and towel rental service in the district. Ever since elementary school, he had a strong desire to contribute to the area. He had participated in the local festival and formed close connections with many local people. As mentioned before, this strong connection between the leader and the people of the local community was key to the success of the development movement.

Mr Ominami was also born and reared in the region and had strong links with many people in the area. He mentioned in the interview that he can chat readily with any senior person in the city and this personality trait was advantageous for realizing the various development projects.

In both cases, motivating regional people to join in the schemes was difficult, so that only individuals with strong connections to the region could advance the movement.

This requirement has universal implications for numerous other regional development programs.

c Concept of renovating regions

In both cases, the social entrepreneurs had an original concept of renovating regions.

Mr Toriyama emphasized the ecological circulation of regional industry. The circulation of businesses vitalizes a town with sustainable development. For such community design, art projects were used to good effect in the initial stage.

Mr Ominami has a strategy of "creative repopulation." This involves attracting in immigrant artists/craftpersons with special skills and using them to reconstruct the regional industries. Even in a modest, remote city, by selling value-added items through real and internet shops, they can create a small but sustainable regional community. In Mr Ominami's thinking, art and crafts are a good tool for vitalizing a region, an idea not unlike those in "Small is Beautiful" by Schumacher (1973).

These two concepts for regional development have many similarities. Neither are aiming at large-scale economic development or development models in the conventional context. They are aiming at small but sustainable development appropriate to the regions. The size of industry in regions should be optimized. Industries in regions are not fixed but must flexibly change to adapt to the current world. Value-added items will be sold in both real and internet shops, and for this reason information technology is one of the keys for regional development. In both cases, because they had no tangible business assets at the first stage, intangible assets in the form of art or art events made good tools for initiating regional development.

7.4.3 Accumulation of social capital as a basis for development

Although the actions of two remarkable social entrepreneurs were essential for regional development, some other conditions were also necessary.

In brief, the accumulation of social capital was vital for both cases.

a Bakuro district

In the case of Bakuro, Mr Toriyama initiated the CET movement. However, for its continuation, the regional people were the main force. It was advantageous that Bakuro is an old part of Tokyo and there were already strong links between people as a result if the summer festival and other cultural events. Most of the residents of the district are people who have been living in the area for a long time, even for several generations. Consequently, once the CET movement got started, a lot of people took part in its activities, for instance, joining in the street parties by providing a barbecue booth or coffee stand: indeed, their energy and passion was crucial. There is no doubt that people's sense of solidarity and the accumulation of social capital were of fundamental value to the success of the movement.

b Kamiyama city

In Kamiyama too, the power of local people was the basis of the movement. In the doll-exchange program, people got together to join the tour to Wilkinsberg. And with both the "Adopt" and the artist-in-residence programs, many people were in support and actively collaborated to make them a success. For all projects, although Mr Ominami established, for instance, organizations like the Green Valley NPO and the centre for international exchange, the involvement of a large number of people was vital for their realization.

The organizational power and energetic input of regional people were consequently essential for the development movement. The accumulation of social capital was again extremely important.

In other words, in both cases, a certain level of accumulated social capital was needed for the movement's success. If there is not a certain level of accumulated social capital in a region, it may well be difficult to realize a development program. So, for regions without an adequate level of social capital, a different approach to development will be necessary, as described in a later chapter.

7.4.4 Assistance by outside agency or local authority

The power of social entrepreneurs and that of the regional community are both important for regional development, as indicated in the previous section. The third factor for a development movement's success is support from outside bodies, including the local authority.

For Bakuro district, the main idea of putting on art events came from people in TDB. As well as the idea, they had the know-how, the detailed knowledge of how to operate the scheme and how to organize relevant people and staff members. The TDB group had already engaged architects, designers and artists as central to their event.

In Kamiyama, the external support by Wilkinsberg in the doll exchange project, help from museum curators and art teachers with the artist-in-residence scheme, and the Tokyo University group input on the "Vacant House" project were all very important. If the development movement had not had this support, it would not have succeeded.

Resource-poor regions do not usually have art specialists or very much knowledge about art, so that for regional development to be prompted by art events, support from outside will always be needed. The social entrepreneur can act as a catalyst, but without support of this kind it would be difficult to proceed.

The support given by local authorities is another key element for the success of development movements.

Because resource-poor regions lack the power to advance themselves, appropriate support by the public authority can be crucial. The word "appropriate" is important here. Local government support in many cases has meant that redevelopment movements lost autonomy. In the case of Kamiyama, Mr Ominami was careful in utilizing such support, as will be described later.

In the case of Bakuro, the trigger for Mr Toriyama to initiate the art event was his joining the committee organizing public occasions to mark the Edo anniversary. For the actual event, they needed the support of police officers with public safety/security matters such as traffic regulation. The initiative of the program was always in the hands of citizens, but backed up by relevant support from public agencies.

In Kamiyama, Mr Ominami established an NPO, and being part of the third sector – neither public not private – made it a suitable platform for the movement. The local authority was always in favor of the projects but it did not have the knowledge to organize them itself. For this reason, citizen initiatives complemented by the support of public bodies was the best way for the movement to proceed.

If the local authority takes complete charge of the movement, the citizen side would lose its autonomy and the movement would fail. The two cases in this chapter give an indication of how there can be collaboration with public bodies in order to advance a development movement. Social entrepreneurs and their colleagues produce the main ideas and retain the initiative, but with the support of the local authority. This was how both these cases operated.

7.4.5 Characteristics of regional development through art

It was not accidental that art events were an effective tool for triggering regional development in these two cases.

As already mentioned, art can be logically positioned as a suitable tool for developing regions which are stagnated due to severe competition by monopolization/oligopolization or globalization. Many resource-poor regions are disadvantaged in terms of lowering costs by mass production or in competition with emerging countries.

In the case of Bakuro, the stagnation of the main industry of the district, clothing retail, was caused by cheap imports from emerging countries. In the case of Kamiyama, the stagnation of the mountain area's main industry, agriculture, was caused by cheaper produce coming in both from other countries and the more fertile domestic plains.

The strategies of lowering costs through the economies of scale associated with mass production or using cheap labor as in emerging countries are generally not available to these resource-poor regions. The opposite strategy, adding value to items by taking particular consumer tastes into account, highlighting originality or art branding, is more relevant for such regions. This would be characterized by small-scale specialist manufacturing or the making of high-value one-off artworks.

In addition, contemporary art is not particularly expensive in Japan and setting up contemporary artwork events can be done for comparatively low cost. Thus, holding contemporary art events is an achievable activity for resource-poor regions without a large budget for development projects.

Art also has a special power to stimulate communication through its emotional impact and can thus be an effective tool for opening up closed communities to interact with the outside world.

7.5 Conclusion

This chapter has focused on two instances of the revitalization and economic development of a resource-poor region. The term "resource-poor" means a region lacks business resources – tangible assets such as advanced technologies, major natural resources or a cultural heritage attractive to tourists. Because of the lack of these tangible assets, it is necessary to develop their intangible assets – in these two cases, by utilizing art.

One case involved the stagnated district, Bakuro, in metropolitan Tokyo. The other involved the stagnated city, Kamiyama, in a remote mountain area of Tokushima prefecture.

The art events project called CET (Central East of Tokyo) in Bakuro and the artist-in-residence project in Kamiyama were described and analyzed. Both projects are part of regional development movements aiming to realize small ecological-style communities characterized by sustainable development through restructuring industries.

Some important conditions were identified as necessary for the success of these programs, as follows.

1 Existence of a committed social entrepreneur with the ability to communicate with the outside world, an affinity with the local community, and a strategic perspective on designing community for sustainable development.
2 Accumulation of social capital as the basis for development.
3 Support by outside bodies and public authorities which respects the initiative and autonomy of regional people.
4 Effective utilization of artwork/art events to trigger regional development.

To confirm these implications and detail the requirements for each condition, further study will be necessary.

Acknowledgments

The author would like to express his sincere thanks to Kazushige Toriyama and Shinya Ominami for agreeing to be interviewed about their activities and their views on community design.

8 Globalization for regional enterprises

8.1 Introduction

For many regions, exchange with the outside world can bring about important opportunities for development. Through the stimulus offered by outsiders, regional people can be energized. It is always said that outsiders are better able to see the strengths or assets of a region, and this may be of value in the branding of regional products. Being aware of fresh thinking and knowledge from the outside world can provide ideas for a region to use in developing its economy.

As has been said, globalization is an important causal factor of regional disparity or regional stagnation in developed countries. In the wave of globalization, all areas face severe industrial competition and resource-poor regions in developed countries find it difficult to compete with emerging countries.

However, globalization is not only a negative factor for regions; it can also be a positive factor if it is utilized as an activating force.

In many regions, a regional leader acts as a window of communication to the outside world. Such leaders gain new ideas for development from the outside world and absorb tacit knowledge from outside people. In this way, their role is that of a kind of conduit between the world inside the community and the world outside.

In this chapter, two interesting cases are described. One is a successful business using the global network for local market purposes. The other is also a successful business, but uses local networks in a global market. Each case suggests a way of opening up a region and pushing it onto the global stage. The rise of globalization cannot be avoided, so it may as well be utilized for regional advance.

Cluster theory, proposed by Porter (1990), is one of the most popular regional development theories. Its main idea is that regional industries can be stimulated by making a kind of industrial cluster in the area, with knowledge links between the competing regional enterprises and knowledge spillover from regional laboratories/universities with regard to advanced technologies. However, the reality in many rural regions in Japan is that they lack such competitive enterprises and they also lack knowledge sources of leading-edge technologies. Even if a knowledge source of advanced technologies does exist, few of the surrounding enterprises can utilize such technologies effectively because most of them are in what we call low-tech industries.

In such a situation, one way to encourage regional industries might be an alliance with companies overseas. Because most domestic enterprises in the same industry are competitors rather than partners, a foreign enterprise far from the domestic market might be more suitable for a business alliance. Inkpen and Ramaswamy (2006) pointed out that, in the last decade, global alliances have become more than price-driven financial relationships shaped by contractual details. Some distinct elements distinguish alliances from other inter-firm relationships, one being the fact that "The relationship involves the exchange of knowledge associated with technologies, skills, or products." In this way the global alliance between enterprises in different countries may compensate for the lack of regional knowledge spillover.

In the next section, a business which successfully utilizes global collaboration in relation to products and technology is introduced, with a view to finding a clue to the solution of stagnated regional economies and regional disparity. The case itself and the analysis of its outstanding business success could suggest strategies for many other rural enterprises and be useful for people who are endeavouring to stimulate regional development.

Another successful example of a regional business will also be described. This enterprise used local networks to build up a production list of items of regional food specialties and extended the business to the global market. In both cases, networking and globalization were vital elements in enterprise development.

8.2 The case of the Nakamura Noen lily business – local business, global network

8.2.1 Introduction

Advanced technology knowledge spillover is thought to be one of the most significant means of encouraging regional industries as well as firming up regional industrial clusters. However, in many rural areas, it is difficult to produce spillover because of lack of an effective knowledge source and lack of the ability of surrounding regional enterprises to make use of such knowledge of this sort.

The case researched here is a lily bulb business in Kochi. Kochi is a rural area with a warm, mild climate, suitable for growing lily bulbs. However, one problem for the industry is the difficulty of selling lily bulbs all the year round because the bulbs cannot be cropped in winter cold. The company's unique idea was to import lily bulbs to Japan, which is in the northern hemisphere, from countries in the southern hemisphere, using refrigerated containers, and ship the bulbs to flower farmers after warming them up. In this way, it could monopolize the winter bulb market in Japan.

This case shows us the importance of finding a competitive business model in rural regions. For this enterprise, global collaboration was an essential element of its business model. Even using conventional technology (low-tech) rather than advanced technology (high-tech), regional industries can be effectively developed by adapting the technology to an appropriate business model. Nakamura Noen (noen means farm) is a unique bulb trading/growing company. Its uniqueness is shown in its business model, which depends on global collaboration, and the way it use technology. The next section introduces an overview of the company and its business scheme.

8.2.2 Overview of Nakamura Noen

The main business of the Nakamura Noen company is to trade and grow lily bulbs for the cut flower industry. It also handles other flowers, such as tulips and freesias.

It currently sells about thirty-four million lily bulbs each year (thirty-two million of which are imported from abroad). It has the majority share of the lily bulb market in Japan. It also sells about 500,000 freesia bulbs and 100,000 tulip bulbs per annum.

It has more than fifty years experience in the bulb business. And now it has grown to be a successful global company, with fifteen employees, annual sales of 2.3 billion yen (in 2007) and a capital value of ninety-nine million yen.

1 History

The founder of the company – the father of the current president, Hiroshi Nakamura – was a high school biology teacher who was always interested in the growing of lilies.

In 1955, he established a business selling lily bulbs in Kochi prefecture. He later transferred the business to his son, who had been worked for an insurance company for twelve years, and who became president of Nakamura Noen in 1998.

In 1984 he initiated the importation of lily bulbs from the Netherlands. That was the first time that Nakamura Noen dealt in bulbs from another country. The reasons for doing so were the greater variety of flower types, the greater choice of items and the lower prices compared to the domestic supply. However, there were strict regulations governing the importation of bulbs from abroad, and it took considerable effort to grow them on in the required manner.

In 1987 Nakumura Noen constructed a refrigerated storage system for the foreign bulbs, and the next year the importation of bulbs was deregulated. So, in 1989, it sent a delegation to the Netherlands to learn about advanced growing techniques as a preparation for enlarging the business of importing foreign bulbs using refrigeration technology.

In 1990 Nakumura Noen became a cooperative to enhance its financial status.

In 1992 they built a heated greenhouse to test-grow bulbs in order to research the best conditions for growing. They also built a facility for warming bulbs cooled down in the refrigerated store.

In 1999, they initiated a new business model involving the importation of lily bulbs from southern hemisphere countries such as Chile and New Zealand, in order to develop a new market in the Japanese winter. Before then, those countries had no tradition of producing lilies, but Nakamura Noen taught them how to grow the bulbs and worked with them as necessary in order to establish the new winter business, for the benefit of all parties. Through these efforts, the company successfully launched the transfer of lily bulbs from countries with an opposite climate.

2 Business model and technology

The Nakamura Noen business model strongly depends on some conventional technologies.

The first of these is the technology of refrigerating natural products. It was not necessary to use any advanced technology like biotechnology. They utilized conventional refrigeration technology for their purpose of shipping bulbs without decomposition. They now receive daily at the port about 200,000 tons of imported bulbs, and they store these bulbs inside the refrigerated store at the company base. The store is kept at a low temperature with a range of only 0.1°C and the thermal system is backed up by an oil generator to ensure its operation even when the electric power supply is interrupted by typhoon or earthquake. The system was purchased from a refrigerator firm; they did not develop it themselves. However, they put a lot of effort into developing the technology to warm up the cooled bulbs themselves, and produced their own special warm bath system for thawing bulbs and encouraging their germination.

The second key technology is that used at the growing stage. In 2007 the company built a large greenhouse of about 1620 m^2. The greenhouse is maintained at between 15°C and 24°C and its daylight hours, ventilation, temperature, water supply and fertilizer application are completely controlled by computer. By using a computerized data system, it is possible to analyze the best conditions to grow bulbs. Because they are dealing with thousands of kinds of bulbs from abroad and the bulbs familiar to Japanese growers make up less than 1 percent of the total, they have to research growing requirements and provide this information to their customers. In a sense, they are not only selling bulbs but also bulb-growing information. This is a key aspect of their success, because the information is extremely valuable to their customers: it effectively differentiates Nakamura Noen from its competitors and gives it a significant competitive advantage.

In other words, the business is not using specially advanced technology (high-tech) but has added their own tacit and explicit knowledge to make conventional technologies (low-tech) their own. This is their innovation style. As is well known, innovation is not only creating a new product with new technology but also some new combination of business elements, like logistics, organization or business style. In this case, the key is the combination of new business model and conventional technologies.

3 Organization management style

The average age of the company's fifteen employees is 32.8. The average salary of the employees is almost twice of that of the average income of people in Kochi prefecture. Of the fifteen employees, one is based in the Netherlands, and ten joined the company after 2001. No employees have left the company. When recruiting a new employee recently, they received numerous applications from other parts of Japan and the ratio of applicants to the position offered was 100 : 1. As shown by such phenomena, the company is extremely attractive to the young.

The president, Hiroshi Nakamura, emphasizes that the basis of management is growing people. He encourages his employees to be independent and make decisions by themselves. He believes that having every employee work independently produces the best service to customers. All the employees participate in the research in the greenhouse to learn how to grow bulbs, as part of company policy.

Even though it is located in a rural area, the company is involved in a flow of international transactions and has foreign visitors every day. The employees are encouraged to improve their foreign language skills. Strong connections with individuals in other countries are a vital element of the company mission.

The president also sees it as important to contribute to the local community, because he sees this community and the human network surrounding the company as another basis of the business. The company organizes a festival for local residents, supports the elementary school and joins in community activities.

4 Impact of external circumstancse on the flower industry

Globalization is not always beneficial for domestic enterprises, because it brings increasingly tough competition. With regard to the flower industry, for instance, the importation of foreign bulbs was deregulated in 1988. Since then, the price of flowers has been falling. For example, a high-value lily which sold for 3000 yen in the 1980s now sells for only one third of that price. Cheap cut flowers from abroad will continue to be imported more and more and Japanese flower growers will fight for their survival.

Nakamura Noen, however, saw the change as a business opportunity and, making use of standard refrigeration technology, developed a unique business model which exploited the freedom to import bulbs.

8.3 The case of Kochi Ice – global business, local network

8.3.1 Overview of Kochi Ice

Kochi Ice is a processed food enterprise which develops, manufactures and sells over thirty kinds of ice cream, using regional products such as yuzu and yamakita oranges, Ikegawa tea, potatoes, tomatoes, Shimanto chestnuts, Tosajiro eggs and sundried salt. The annual sales are about 400 million yen (US$4 million) and there are about twenty employees. They make around 30,000 ice creams a day. Five people work in the factory on a double shift system. The factory is extremely clean and there is an air-shower system at the entrance. The mixing of materials and the packaging of ice creams is automized.

> Current sales depend mainly (95 percent) on urban markets like Tokyo, and the business's high-price, high-quality products are targeted at the urban consumer. One reason for hed regional ice-cream manufacturer, and another is that the urban market is larger than the regional market.

Because ice cream is a seasonal item, mainly purchased in summer, Kochi Ice is looking to develop markets in countries/continents that are hot during the Japanese winter season – for instance, Singapore, Hong Kong, Taiwan, Indonesia, Africa, and the Middle East. The business is confident that it can successfully develop these new markets. The president travels to these countries and visits their retail outlets himself. He sells Kochi Ice items at the front of the shop and chats with customers to learn what they think – even though his foreign language skills are limited.

They pay a lot of attention to the taste of their products. "Taste is everything," the president said. They search all over the region of Kochi for suitable new ingredients for their ice cream. Once they find a good food material, they contract to buy directly from the producer in order to reduce costs and maintain active communication with their farm suppliers. They value long-term relationships with the farms, to "grow" them and ensure taste and quality. Because Kochi Ice can use misshapen products, farms are very happy to sell to them, and the sales can increase their incomes by up to 40 percent. This win-win strategy makes for successful collaboration with regional farms. The business employs many techniques for enhancing its ice-cream flavours, for instance, adding orange zest for its rich quality, selecting a particular tomato variety for sweetness, and using food materials produced specially in the region to extend its range.

They have now introduced an internet retail system. They have received orders for up to 1300 ice creams over three days though this new service.

In 2011, their ice cream was selected as No. 1 in the sorbet category by the Nikkei newspaper.

8.3.2 History of the enterprise

The Kochi Ice business depends very much on the personality of the current president and the founder of the enterprise, Fumiya Hamamachi.

Mr Hamamachi grew up the second son of a fisherman, and became a fisherman himself after graduating from junior high school. He got married when he was twenty-one years old, and he then quit fishing and became a salesperson for a movie-making enterprise in the city.

In 1985, this enterprise set up a food department and started selling an ice cream named Ice Kurin to department stores outside the prefecture. Mr

Hamamachi worked as a salesperson in this division for three years. He travelled all over the country to promote the ice cream at regional product exhibitions. He said he participated in over 300 of these exhibitions a year at that time. Even though the item was not particularly popular and was difficult to sell, he secured over 300 customers in many parts of Japan.

In 1988 the enterprise decided to dealing in ice cream. However, Mr Hamamachi did not want to give up selling it because he now had so many customers. He therefore left his employment and started up his own business selling ice cream. He borrowed 400,000 yen (about US$4000) from an insurance company, bought a large refrigerated truck to carry the ice cream, and embarked upon sales tours all over the country. He experienced a great deal of hardship during this period. However, he learnt how to sell items by taking account of customers' preferences, and he learnt the importance of personal links with customers. "Don't give up: if you don't beat the drum, you can't hear the sound of the drum" was how his mother expressed his philosophy of the time. Later, he enjoyed drawing and writing to express his view of life, remembering this period.

In 1989 NHK, the Japanese public broadcasting organisation, made a program about the Shimanto river in Kochi, describing it as the cleanest river in Japan. This started a Kochi boom, but although there was a lot of interest in the place, Kochi did not have many local processed foods and thus could not take proper advantage of the business opportunity. Mr Hamamachi therefore decided to make ice cream by himself and went to Yokohama to learn about the manufacturing process.

In 1995 he built a factory in Kochi and established his own enterprise, "Kochi Ice", producing speciality ice creams using local ingredients.

In 2002 he met a well-known designer named Makoto Umebara. Mr Umebara had a particular gift for raising the profile of regional products through successful packaging design and advertizing copy. Mr Hamamachi asked him to design new packaging for his ice cream. Mr Umebara came up with: "Ice cream made in Tosa [the original name of Kochi]" and "This company is always seeking delicious new ingredients for its ice cream," and designed elegant yellow packaging.

As predicted by Mr Umebara, the annual sales of Kochi Ice tripled within three years.

In 2004 Mr Hamamachi moved the factory to Inocho and increased production. Now annual sales are in the region of 400 million yen (about US$4 million) and he has hired a chef to develop a new confectionery line.

8.4 Analysis and discussion

8.4.1 Global network for local market

In the case of Nakamura Noen, the business model can be characterized as utilizing the global network for a local market.

As described, the Nakamura Noen business strongly depends on importing lily bulbs. Over 90 percent of the lily bulbs it deals in are imported. This success story is an example of how rural enterprises can overcome difficult circumstances. The point is that they created a business model to utilize globalization positively.

The most outstanding feature of the business model is the importation of lily bulbs from countries in the southern hemisphere. By this means they were able to monopolize the winter lily market in Japan. In the past there were very limited sales of lilies in winter because of the difficulty of growing lily bulbs or flowers in the cold. Nakamura Noen came up with the idea of developing this market. It is a good example of how globalization can bring about market innovation. In this case, Nakamura Noen built up a global network for purchasing the materials for his products, and in this way gained a very large share in the domestic market.

Nakamura Noen also developed close links with Dutch bulb growers and exchanged information about lilies and other flowers. It collaborated with its foreign producers and learnt about their specialist cultivation techniques; they then passed this information on to their many farm customers in Japan via the Nakamura Noen website.

In addition, they conducted their own research on the optimum growing conditions for lily bulbs by building a large greenhouse and collecting data on water, temperature/humidity, fertilizer and ventilation requirements, using a computer-controlled system. The business sells bulbs to lily farmers together with information about growing conditions. It is creating its own additional value, which is the strength of the enterprise. And the global network is a very effective element in their business model. The Nakamura Noen style of business could be relevant for many enterprises, not only in rural areas but also in towns and cities.

Their business model is schematically described in Figure 8.1.

This diagram of their business model shows that they are transacting not only bulbs but also knowledge about bulbs through global collaboration. This proved key to their business success because the knowledge linkage became their core competence in the field.

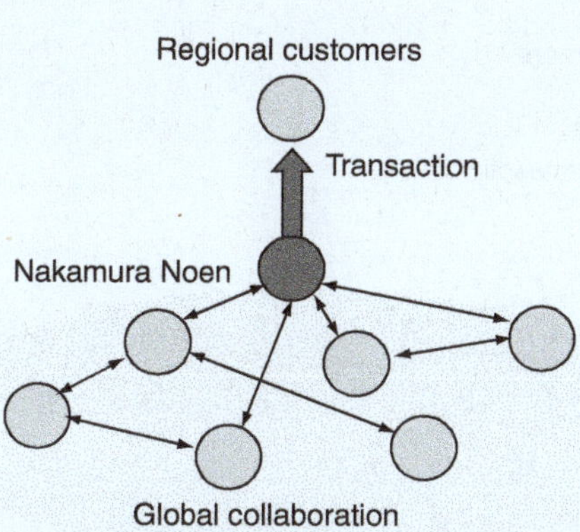

Figure 8.1 Business model based on global networks.

8.4.2 Local network for global market

By contrast, the business model of Kochi Ice may be characterized as utilizing the local network for a global market.

The strength of the enterprise originates in the close connections it has developed with its many regional farm producers of speciality foodstuffs. Mr Hamamchi, the president, visited in person numerous farms, and discussed arrangements with them as part of establishing good long-term relationships. Based on these personal links, he was able to develop many different ice creams with special regional flavours. The primary strength of the business is, of course, the taste of the ice cream and its quality.

But the main market of this enterprise is not the region but urban areas in Japan and other countries. The local market is very small because of depopulation and aging. Thus, the strategy of this enterprise is entirely rational. By respecting the uniqueness and quality of regional food materials and creating new items with special regional flavours, the enterprise is able to target urban and global markets.

Kochi Ice is an instance of another type of survival strategy for regional enterprises in a globalized world. It made use of globalization, but in a different manner to Nakamura Noen. Both cases indicate, however, that regional enterprises must positively utilize globalization if they are to survive in the modern world.

8.5 Conclusion

The cases of Nakamura Noen and Kochi Ice showed us examples of successful local businesses. Their success depended on the following.

1 Utilizing global network and collaborating with local market
2 Utilizing local network and collaborating with global market

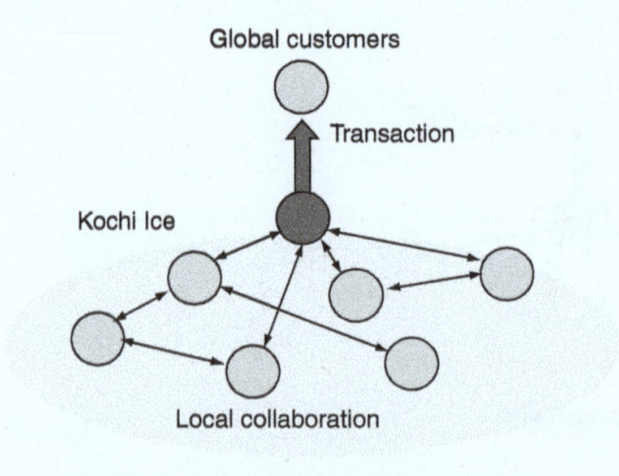

Figure 8.2 Business model based on local networks.

The cases suggest that many rural enterprises without substantial capital or other resources could establish successful business by utilizing global or local networks to penetrate the local or global market. The key to the survival of regional enterprises in the present globalized world is building a business model which approaches global/local network/collaboration positively. To stimulate regional industry, the most urgent requirement may be business leaders able to develop business models which take the globalized world into account. Also, other examples of success should be made known, to act as a source of ideas for regional people.

Acknowledgments

The author would like to express his sincere appreciation to President Hiroshi Nakamura and the staff of Nakanmura Noen for their kind cooperation in interviews. Thanks are also due to President Tastuya Hamamachi and the staff of Kochi Ice for their kind cooperation in interviews.

9 An experiment in regional development through ecological business

9.1 Introduction

To gain proper insight into the issue of regional development, it is not sufficient to gather data only as an observer. For this reason we decided to establish a non-profit organization (NPO), Tosa Arts & Crafts, as a vehicle for regional development efforts of our own. In parallel to the conventional research described in earlier chapters, we explored the basic issues of and real obstacles to regional development through actual practice. Taking into account what had been learnt from observations, we designed a methodology and framework for our activities, and evaluated the results to feed back into further planning. Through the cycle of planning, practice, checking and evaluation – just as in ordinary business – we could achieve an ever-deeper analysis. In this sense, the NPO project was a kind of experimental demonstration of theories and implications.

9.2 Designing the Tosa Arts & Crafts project

There are many ways of approaching regional revitalization and regional economic development. Figure 9.1 is a schematic view of regional development which focuses on asset flow.

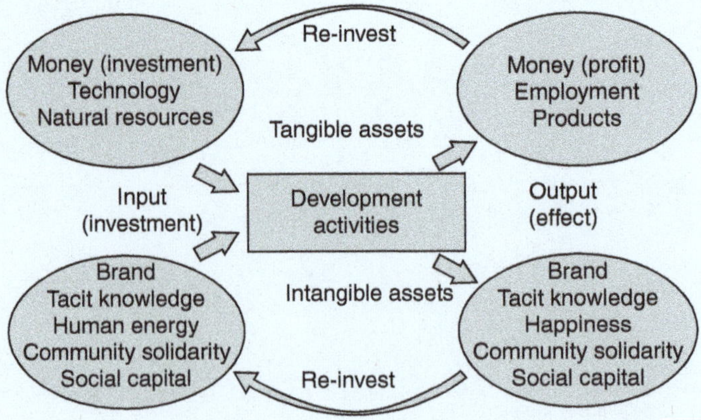

Figure 9.1 Asset flow in development activities (some tangible assets).

Tangible assets (such as natural resources, capital and technology) and intangible assets (such as social capital in the form of human vitality, tacit knowledge and community solidarity) are used as business resources for regional development activities, in order to acquire tangible gains (such as profit, employment and economic advantage) and intangible gains (such as regional branding, the greater happiness of local people, mental liveliness and an accumulation of social capital). Some of the output might be reinvested, as shown in the figure.

In ordinary manufacturing activity, tangible assets like capital, materials and technology are mainly invested in for the purpose of a tangible output like financial profit. In some businesses, the output might be an intangible asset such as brand, but if the brand value is reinvested into the business, there will be further financial gain.

In some types of business, tangible asset output (financial gain) is generated by solely inputting intangible assets (such as art or human effort), as shown in Figure 9.2.

If we consider development activities in resource-poor rural regions, it would seem desirable that the input focus should be on intangible assets because, by definition, such areas do not have many tangible assets as business resources.

The basic idea for regional development in our project was to make use of intangible assets rather than tangible assets.

Kochi prefecture ranks poorly in terms of GDP and average household income compared to other prefectures in Japan. It has the problem of stagnated industries. In addition, the profitability of agriculture is low in the dominant mountain areas and other industries are largely inactive in these parts. The outflow of young people accelerates depopulation and aging, and the consequent reducing labor force and shrinking consumer market puts further pressure on the regional economy. Long-term economic stagnation has had a generally depressing effect and led to a deterioration of solidarity and collaborative activity within communities.

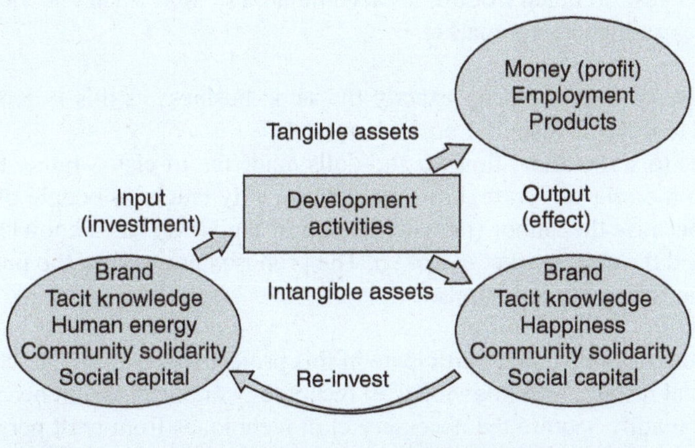

Figure 9.2 Asset flow in development activities (resource-poor).

To seek to overcome these problems in Kochi, we needed to develop a project which would motivate and stimulate people. The ideal requirements for such a project are as follows.

1 Participation possible for people without specific abilities, financial resources or experience of technology or management.
2 Work activity not requiring great physical strength which can be practiced at home even by housewives and the elderly.
3 Quickly generated cash income.
4 Contributing to regional branding and the recovery of regional people's self-confidence.
5 Ready establishment in the region and difficultly in being replicated elsewhere.

If the project should satisfy all these requirements, it would be very advantageous for regional revitalization and the development of rural areas.

The Irodori business project was thought of as ideal in these respects.

The Irodori enterprise sold leaves gathered in the mountains by senior citizens from the village to exclusive Japanese restaurants. The business may be characterized as follows.

1 Many village people were able to participate in the project without specific abilities, financial resources or knowledge of technology or management (apart from knowledge of the regional mountains).
2 People in their eighties and nineties and housewives could work with ease in their own homes because leaves are extremely light.
3 Cash income was quickly generated, with some participants being paid on a daily basis.
4 The success of the business led to a higher profile for Kamikatsu city (i.e. regional branding) and regional people's greater self-confidence.
5 It was readily established in the region, and other areas could not easily compete because so much Irodori has accumulated so much tacit knowledge about leaves and the leaves market.

We could not, of course, set up exactly the same business as this in Kochi, but we decided to develop a similar business model.

The idea was to sell crafts – flowers and dolls made out of clay – rather than leaves, because the relevant craft skills could be quickly taught to people of all ages and also because the author (the chairperson of the NPO) has a knowledge of both crafts and the craft market in Tokyo. The proposed project had the potential to satisfy the following conditions.

1 Many regional people could participate in this project without specific abilities, financial resources or knowledge of technology or management because they could readily acquire the necessary craft techniques from craft persons and artists.

2 Older people and housewives could work at the project in their own homes because ceramic flowers and dolls are compact and light and convenient to handle.
3 Cash income could be generated quickly through the direct sales of participants' artworks.
4 If successful, the project would contribute to regional branding and the greater self-confidence of regional people.
5 It would be readily established in the region and would be impossible to precisely replicate elsewhere. Artworks are by their nature original, so all regions could develop some kind of uniqueness through their own artworks. The project could be duplicated elsewhere; however, people in other areas would always be creating another originality.

As already mentioned, the advantage of using arts and crafts is that they encourage originality linked to what can be termed regional brand. As discussed in Chapters 4 and 8, art has a special power to vitalize regions. In contrast to mass production, making artwork is about limited editions and consequently lends itself to branding for niche markets. Art and craftworks will become special regional products and their sale as souvenirs a useful source of regional income. This kind of business project is unlikely to make a large amount of money or grow into a major industry, but it has the potential to be adequate for a modest number of rural people and that is its purpose.

Based on these points, the articles of association of the NPO were defined as follows.

1 Purpose of the NPO

The purpose of this NPO is public service, to create job opportunities and income for residents of mountain areas, craft persons, housewives, unemployed and handicapped persons in the region, by means of education in traditional art and craft techniques, the development and sale of special regional products, and the planning and execution of art events.

2 Activities of the NPO

In order to achieve this purpose, the NPO is active in the following fields: economic development, community development, vocational education, job creation, and culture, art and sport research.

The case studies in Chapters 6 to 8 showed the importance of leadership in regional business development. A regional leader provides a window to the outside world and unites local people through his/her community affiliations. With Tosa Arts & Crafts, the author and chairperson of the NPO could act as a window to the outside world but, because he was born and grew up outside the region, was not in a position to unites the local community through existing connections. However, if no action was taken until all the conditions for success were met, little would ever be initiated, and it is important to initiate something even if the situation is less than perfect. While taking action, we should think how best to fulfill the conditions for success. This is the policy of the NPO.

9.3 Activities in the first year

In 2010, its first year, the NPO undertook the following.

1 Craft education and the sale of work

The NPO invited a well-known ceramic artist, who had frequently exhibited in Tokyo and had a successful sales record, to teach ceramic-flower techniques (see Figure 9.3) to a large class of local people, including junior high school students and senior citizens.

We also recruited university student volunteers to help with the event and educated them in event management practice. A selling exhibition of the artwork produced was held in Kochi city centre. The exhibition was intended to show regional people that they could earn money this way (see Figure 9.4).

2 Promotion of a regional product overseas

In the Kochi town of Tosayamada, there is a traditional regional item called a furafu. It is a kind of flag used to celebrate a boy's health and development on a certain day in May. It is decorated with colorful drawings of Samurai knights. We

Figure 9.3 Ceramic flowers.

Figure 9.4 The exhibition of ceramic flowers in Kochi city.

brought some furafu to souvenir shops and department stores in London and asked if they would be interested in selling them. Most of them agreed to take some.

We also visited some universities in Wales and made arrangements for them to exhibit traditional furafu in their gallery spaces, and some overseas Japanese students suggested they could promote the project in their own colleges. In this way, the scheme prompted new relationships between the universities of Japan and the UK.

9.4 Reflections on the first year and activities in the second year

At the start of 2011, we reflected on the impact of the first year's activities.

Our analysis was that we had misunderstood the thinking of regional people. For example, regarding the teaching of ceramic techniques, few senior citizens were familiar with ceramic flowers and they did not become interested in them. And other attendees of the class were not interested in learning the technique as a means to earn money because most of them were perfectly well off. These misunderstandings originated in the lack of pre-existing connections between NPO members and people in the region. Thus, adding an individual with good regional affiliations to the organization became the first priority for the NPO in its second year. This strategy was based on what was learnt from the cases examined in Chapter 8.

1 Inviting Tatsuya Hamada into the NPO and a new art project

Tatsuya Hamada was born in Shimanto in Kochi and grew up in the city. He moved to Tokyo to work in an event planning enterprise when he was twenty but later returned to Kochi to contribute to his home area. He was made aware of the power of art through some events run by the prefectural museum, which used an empty school for the venue.

In 2009 he initiated the Okino Island Art Project. This was an art event aimed at vitalizing a depopulated, remote island, using some vacant houses and schools. He invited some artists from the region and some from Tokyo to exhibit their work, and around twenty people took part.

In 2010, the second year of the Okino Island Art Project, the range of participants was enlarged through the universities. Suguru Kwashima, a master's student at Kochi University of Technology, joined the project and because his major was architecture, the departmental professor (Professor Yoshida) and other architecture students initiated a research project on the island. In addition, some female students from the prefectural University of Kochi became involved due to their interest in the traditional dishes of Okino and (neighboring) Uguru island. The number of people taking part in the project grew to around forty.

Figures 9.5 and 9.6 show something of Uguru in 2010. The island's population was once as high as 400 and most islanders were engaged in fishing bonitos. When the bonito fishery collapsed, the population fell to just twenty-two and the elementary school and the junior high school both closed. Nowadays, most of the islanders are in their seventies or eighties and the only shop is a vending machine for soft drinks. On the hill there was a ruined school gymnasium, as shown in Figure 9.7.

Figure 9.5 The harbor on Uguru island.

Figure 9.6 Houses on Uguru island.

Figure 9.7 The school gymnasium in 2010 before the start of renovation work.

The volunteer students attached to the project renovated this building and turned it into a gallery for contemporary art (see Figure 9.8). They put together an art exhibition (see Figure 9.9) to attract tourists from outside, and more than 100 visitors came to the island as a result.

By inviting Mr Hamada to become a core member of Tosa Arts & Crafts, the activities of the Okino Island Art Project and those of the NPO were merged. By including Mr Hamada, the NPO's connection to the region was very much enhanced and this proved extremely beneficial.

In 2011, the island project was added to by still more participants. Maiko Iwata, an artist, and Subaru Nakatsugawa, a novelist, both from Tokyo, brought some unusual ideas to the project. Mr Nakatsugawa wrote a mystery novel, "The Golden Legend of Rukuru Island," with Uguru island as the mystery's virtual stage. The idea is that readers upload a guide to the mystery tour from the website and register to join. Members of the tour then come to Uguru in the summer and visit different places on the island to get clues, as in role-playing games, with the mystery solved on the final day.

Numerous university students and graduates acted characters in the play on the island, to make it all seem real.

Other students cooked for the tourists as part of the hospitality offered. The tour drama was made into a movie, with English narration, and uploaded on to the internet.

By using art and the internet, a small island with the population of only twenty-two came to be known to a lot of people.

Figure 9.8 The school gymnasium in the process of being transformed into an art gallery.

Figure 9.9 An artwork installed in the gallery.

In 2011, the total number of people related to the whole program came to more than sixty. The reason why so many people participated in some way was that there was a loose linkage of a variety of people with a variety of intentions. The artists in Tokyo were interested in the mystery tour as an art event, the university students majoring in architecture were interested in architecture research on an island, the female students were interested in developing the islands' historical dishes, and other volunteer students were just enjoying the project activity and chatting with elderly island people. The lack of a tight formal structure and the diversity of intentions allowed a larger number of people to be involved than might have been the case.

In this increase in the number of participants, the autonomy of each group is thought to be important. Each of the groups operated independently and respected the independence of the other groups: there was a degree of synergy. With regard for relationships with the islanders, all the students related to the islanders in a different way. The architecture students called at houses to interview residents about their lifestyle; the women listened to elderly ladies to learn more about their traditional dishes; and the media students dropped in to houses to take pictures of the islanders. They made contact with islanders in many different ways and it was so good for deepen the linkage with islanders.

The islanders themselves said that it was enjoyable to chat with the many young students, so like their grandsons and granddaughters. They also said that their main wish was not to be rich but that traditional culture and customs should be respected. We learnt from this project the very important rule that regional development should be practiced according to the real desires of regional people.

2 Shimanto-Inverness exchange project

By adding Mr Hamada to their group, the NPO gained a strong link to Shimanto city. The NPO decided to set up friendship or "twinning" links between Shimanto and some cities in other countries, as a way of opening up the regional community to the outside world, another strategy learnt from the case studies. The idea was to establish an exchange scheme between Shimanto and Inverness, a city in Scotland. Shimanto and Inverness were chosen because both cities have legendary creatures living in water, Nessy and Kappa. According to the legend, Nessy lives in Lough Ness and looks like an ancient dinosaur. Kappa lives in the Shimanto river and resembles a human with green skin and a plate on its head. Taking these legends as a unifying theme, the NPO proposed that the two cities collaborate over an art event.

The plan was to exchange the work of artists from each city in PDF form, printing it out in order that joint or simultaneous exhibitions might be held in Shimanto and Inverness. The emailing of artwork means that the project does not need to invest any significant money. The mayor of Shimanto was willingly to support the scheme and the first exhibition is scheduled for March 2012.

3 Producing filmed documentaries

Some students suggested making filmed documentaries of the various projects. No professional people were involved but, using iMovie software, a record of NPO activities was successfully completed. Video is an accessible communication tool and the filmed record meant that the NPO's work could be readily understood by a lot of people, and local people felt proud. By adding English narration, video can be also be used to communicate with people in other countries. This video was shown to people in Inverness and served to promote the exchange project.

9.5 Analysis and discussion

As a result of examining the cases in Chapters 4 to 9, a number of conclusions have been reached regarding regional development through ecological business or art, particularly where it involves resource-poor rural areas.

In summary, there are some basic conditions for success.

1. An accumulation of social capital in the region in terms of community solidarity, collaborative power, join-mission, mutual respect and sense of identity. If the amount of accumulated social capital is small, it will be difficult to establish regional development activities.
2. A regional leader, as social entrepreneur, should have a good affinity with

the regional community and use this connection to bring about knowledge transfer between the community and the outside world – acting as a communication bridge. If the arts or a specific kind of business are the main means of development, he/she will need to have some relevant knowledge in those areas.

In addition, a regional leader and social entrepreneur should have ideas about designing community for sustainable development. They might have relevant expertise in planning events or in business, marketing or community development, with a proper long-term perspective.

Figure 9.10 shows these conditions for development in diagrammatic form.

The significance of regional leaders has been made clear. However, the reality is that many regions do not have a leader, or, if they do have a leader, he/she is not able to exert sufficient influence. Thus, in many areas, support for development from the outside world is of great importance.

Although some accumulation of social capital will always be needed for the establishment of businesses or putting on of art events, in many instances the power of regional people is so weak that the support of public offices or the outside world is crucial. Indeed, support from the outside world – what may be termed horizontal collaboration – can make a critical difference to the success of initiatives in many regions, as shown in Figure 9.11.

As mentioned in section 9.3, if we wait until we can satisfy all the conditions for successful regional development, we will not initiate anything. It is important to take some action whether the situation is hopeful or not. But alongside this action, we should think how best to meet the conditions for success.

With Tosa Arts & Crafts, even after only one year the importance of having real connections to the local community was recognized. For this reason we took the strategic decision to ask Mr Hamada to join the NPO as a regional leader. However, if we had not already initiated some NPO activities and gathered some

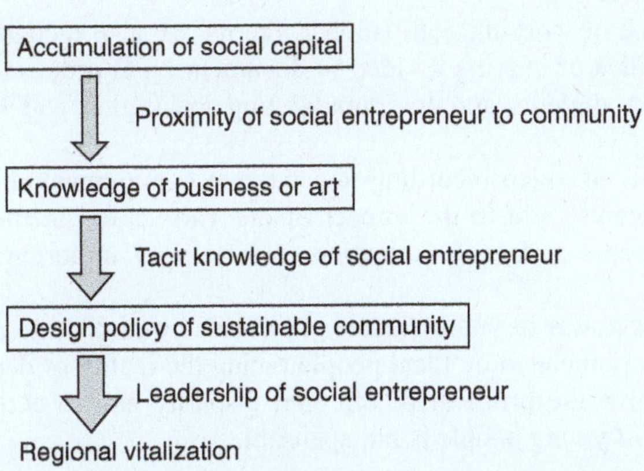

Figure 9.10 General conditions for regional development.

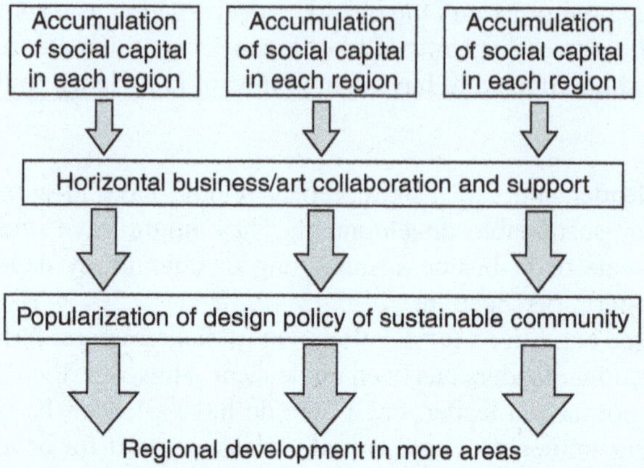

Figure 9.11 Horizontal collaboration to extend regional development to new areas.

results, a partnership would not have been viable. In other words, no activity is worthless and all effort contributes to regional people's advance.

The actual development activities of Tosa Arts & Crafts consisted of both elements – the vertical power of regional community and regional leader, and the horizontal power of support from the outside world. Even with our modest NPO projects we came to understand the importance of having both in place.

After only two years, the number of participants had significantly grown. The experience of the Uguru island project showed that the loose linkage of individuals and groups is an effective way to increase the numbers involved. By respecting the autonomy of each person/group, the development activities become extensive and diverse. We also learned, through bringing together Inverness and Shimanto, that it is stimulating for regions to exchange with regions in other countries. Establishing links beyond the border will effect regional development in any circumstance.

Through the experience of working with student interns, we also recognized the value of media. The idea of making a video to document NPO projects was useful both for educating students and for popularizing the region and NPO activities.

By combining the tools of video recording and internet communication, we were able to very significantly add to the impact of our various engagements. For this reason, using media and communication tools is very important for regional development.

We also recognized the power of young people. The visits by students to rural villages were very much appreciated by local people facing the reality of depopulation and aging. To solve the problem of regional disparity and to activate regions, the participation of young people is indispensable.

10 Summary

10.1 The case studies

Between Chapter 4 and Chapter 9, around twenty cases were described and analyzed. The discussions and conclusions are summarized as follows.

In Chapter 4, the two cases both involved regional development through the organization of art events. Art events proved an effective tool for stimulating and raising the spirits of regional people. The first case was an unusual instance of a temporary museum on the seashore of a rural area. People in the region established this museum with a very small budget and without destroying the area's natural environment. The success of the activity was due to local people's strong hometown feelings and their respect for regional culture and in fact the main effect of the activity was also what could be called spiritual rather than economic. In the second case, the art event had a very significant impact in both social/spiritual and economic terms. More than 500,000 people visited remote, mountainous areas over the three months of the event; however, a budget of several hundred million yen was necessary. The two cases indicate the importance of social/spiritual/emotional elements as well as financial support in regional development. Further, regional development itself appears to consist of two elements: revitalizing people and generating economic improvement. Both elements are important, at least one is indispensable and they compliment each other: it is a harmonious relationship.

The cases also suggest that localization and globalization can be complimentary. Valuing local culture is important for regional development, but so is interaction with people beyond the region and the stimulation offered by the outside world. Again, there is not necessarily any conflict: rather, their productive harmonization may be essential for successful regional development.

In Chapter 5, six cases were described, with the focus on how they developed ecological businesses without conventional business resources.

The first part of the chapter looked at three businesses utilizing natural resources. One was a business selling leaves from trees in the mountains to high-end traditional restaurants in metropolitan areas, to decorate dishes. Another was a business selling wood shavings from forestry operations to urban consumers in the form of scent bags for the bath. The third was a business selling juice made from misshapen citrus fruits grown around a small village in the heart of mountains to urban consumers. These three cases have in common the imbuing of items without worth in the conventional context with associations of a rural "natural life", and selling to urban consumers. That is, they show that rural life itself can have a value, particularly for urban people living modern lives. In addition, all three businesses were sustainable in terms of care for the natural environment and beneficial for both rural and urban communities. These cases suggest ways in which rural and urban peoples can co-exist and co-evolve.

Some other cases were also described in the chapter. A business which utilized dialect as a business resource, a business turning a sinking island and shallow sea into an image of old-fashioned peace to attract tourists, and a business making cosmetic products from fish scales were discussed in the context of using resources usually thought to have no commercial worth. Their ideas are relevant for innovatory sustainable development.

In Chapter 6, several cases were described from the viewpoint of regional community as a platform for regional business. Three cases representing different business scales and different community areas were subjected to comparative analysis. Despite these contrasts, all three successful regional businesses were drawing on the solidarity of regional people, based on hometown feelings and/or respect for regional culture, for their business models. That is, the cases suggest that hometown feelings and respect for regional culture are in themselves valuable intangible assets for business development. These intangible assets are usually termed social capital. The cases indicate that, even with a large enterprise in a metropolitan area, social, moral and national culture can be an important business resource. The case of the regional hospital also showed that social networking in order to share information and tacit knowledge was a significant part of establishing a successful regional business. Another aspect of this was evaluated in Chapter 8.

In Chapter 7, two cases of redesigning and renovating regional community were analyzed. As mentioned in Chapter 4, art can be a convenient and effective tool for socially/spiritually stimulating regional people, particularly in resource-poor regions. The two cases described in this chapter utilized art events for vitalizing regions both socially and economically. Moreover, they renovated regions with a view to sustainable development. The role of regional leaders as social entrepreneurs was significant. These individuals were a source of outside knowledge and acted as a bridge to the outside world for their local communities. The social entrepreneurs' strong connections with their communities, combined with support from the outside world and/or local authorities, were important for the success of the programs.

In Chapter 8, the discussion of Chapter 6 was extended. In Chapter 6 we learned that regional human networks were important for regional development, but human connections with the outside world are also important, particularly for survival in the modern world. In this chapter, two contrasting cases were illustrated from the point of view of globalization. The first case was an instance of global networks/collaboration used for local and domestic markets. An enterprise dealing in lily bulbs utilized global links to add value to items sold in

Japan. The second case utilized local networks and local collaboration for the global market. The processed food enterprise, Kochi Ice, developed numerous delicious ice creams, working closely with local farms to penetrate a global market. In both cases, networking took place in the context of globalization. And through these human networks, tacit knowledge as well as explicit knowledge was shared as a weapon for survival.

In both cases, communicating with people in the globalized world was key to advancing regional business. The idea of utilizing outside strength has great potential for many regional people. The head of an enterprise is the key person to link regional business and the outside world, as discussed in Chapter 7.

Another element of the business success of these cases was selling products with a value-added information service based on close communication with customers. Tangible assets are not essential for business success if intangible assets are created and/or utilized.

In Chapter 9 there was an account of a practical experiment in regional development which drew on what had been learnt from the case studies. An NPO, Tosa Arts & Crafts, was established in 2010, aimed at developing a resource-poor rural area through making and selling crafts and putting on art events for regional branding and tourism.

The experience of the first year confirmed the importance of having local connections. Thus, in the second year, a person with strong affiliations with the area was added to the NPO, and the range of its activities was enlarged. Through a system of loose linkages, a large number of people and groups participated in development activities on remote, depopulated Uguru island. A role-playing mystery tour was organized, involving the collaboration of a novelist, artists, university students and residents, part of promoting a tiny island with a population of only twenty. A variety of the arts, including written fiction, drama, film, drawing, sculpture, music and dance were used in this program. And the internet was also a highly effective tool. The total cost, however, was so low that the project can be continued for many years.

These case studies show the potential for business of intangible assets such as hometown feelings, respect for local culture, community solidarity, human networks and shared tacit knowledge, the rural lifestyle and communication with outsiders, the use of which does not destroy the natural environment like most conventional mass production schemes. Of course, the scale of most of the rural businesses was small, their markets tended to be niche and their profit and economic impact were generally limited. However, we can conclude the following:

- a The development goals of people in the regions were not only economic but also intellectual, social and spiritual – indeed, the harmonization of economic and mental satisfactions.
- b These modest businesses, artistic activities and lives in the regions complemented lives in urban areas where most people are involved in conventional, mass-production business operations. In that sense, urban lives and rural lives may be harmonized.

10.2 Leadership and community in relation to knowledge management

The analysis of the case studies showed up the vital contribution of key individuals in many rural businesses. It has been frequently pointed out that the role of leader is extremely important in rural enterprises and rural communities. Most resource-poor rural regions lack human resources in general and community leaders in particular because of depopulation, aging and the stagnation of local industry. In addition, most communities in such areas are somewhat closed and consequently lack information about building new types of business enterprise. In particular they lack opportunities to acquire new tacit knowledge, including new business know-how, from the outside world. Thus, most of the business/community leaders in rural regions are people who can be a window to the outside world, even physically moving between their own community and the outside world. These leaders are good at communicating with both local people and outside people and good at sharing tacit knowledge through their connections. In other words, they act as catalysts, as shown schematically in Figure 10.1.

These leaders also act as a bridge between local people and outside people, as shown schematically in Figure 10.2. Put another way, the role of a leader is to be a kind of window to the outside world for a region's people. This role and the leader's characteristics are different from the conventional view of leaders exerting strong centralized control over people.

As a result of the activities of such leaders, if regional communities have sufficient strength and flexible enough organizations to enable them to share their tacit knowledge, they can establish new businesses based on the infrastructure of human networks. We may call such an infrastructure a business platform for regional people. A platform based on the sharing of tacit knowledge will be more effective for business establishment than a platform which only shares explicit knowledge, as schematically indicated in Figure 10.3.

Through analyzing the cases described in Chapters 4 to 9, we learnt the importance of leadership and community for business establishment – and sustainable community development – in rural regions, and saw how human factors are

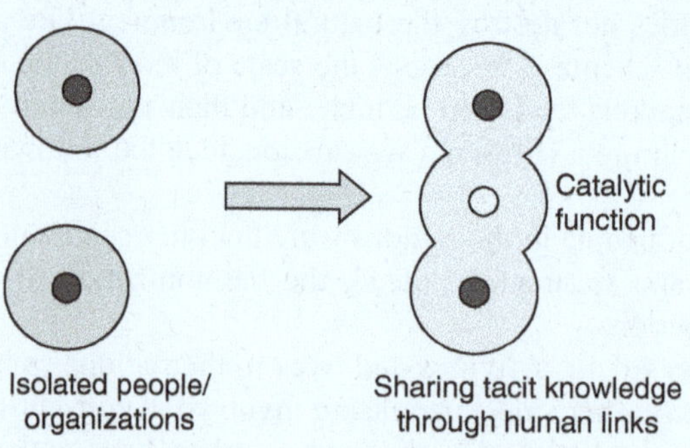

Figure 10.1 Leader as catalyst, connecting people and business.

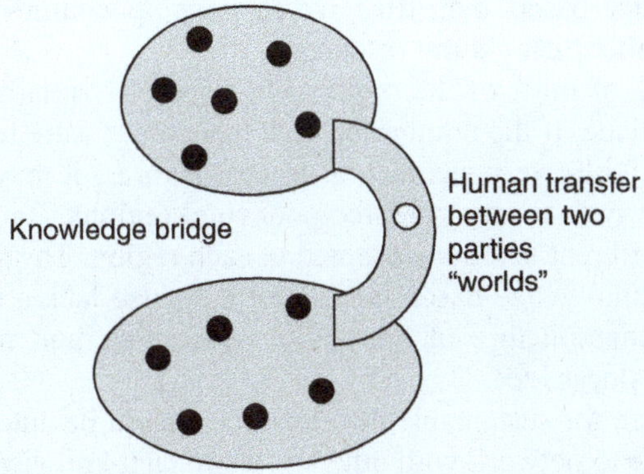

Figure 10.2 Leader as knowledge bridge between outside and inside communities.

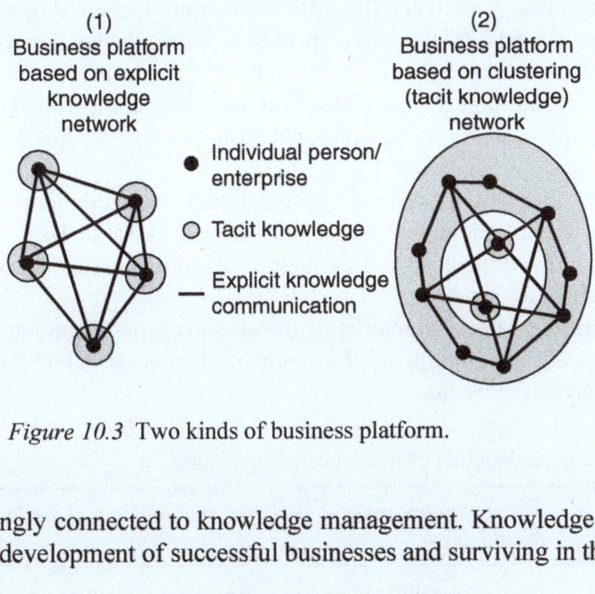

Figure 10.3 Two kinds of business platform.

strongly connected to knowledge management. Knowledge management is key to the development of successful businesses and surviving in the modern world.

10.3 Innovation for sustainable development

The analysis of diverse business cases in resource-poor rural regions has clarified the characteristics of innovation for sustainable development.

Instead of utilizing large amounts of natural resources, investment money, large factories or other material resources, many resource-poor rural regions have developed businesses which recycle used materials and give new value to "useless" materials. They have sometimes developed information as a value-added commodity, or found a new value for "natural" life in the country as a respite from urban life. The resources are non-limited because most can be utilized without any destruction of the natural environment. In this sense, they are not dissimilar to knowledge-based industries which develop commercial values based on information rather than natural resources.

Although the business scale of most of the regional businesses is relatively modest and their markets are niche, if the number of such businesses were to be multiplied their total effect could be very significant. In other words, it may be impossible to find one single way to rescue resource-poor rural regions. Rather, there is a need for numerous different solutions adapted to each region. The situation is somewhat similar for knowledge-based industries: they also lack a universal direction, such as the manufacture of household necessities, and must each come up with a unique business idea.

People involved in innovation for sustainable development should be autonomous and decentralized but able to network with others to share tacit knowledge. The organization of knowledge-based industries may be similar: decentralized, with flexible communication – a little like a village.

Small communities need to introduce new knowledge from the outside world, and some leaders act as a bridge between the different communities and open up a window to the outside world. They move in person between the two communities and bring back tacit knowledge to share with their community.

This suggests the potential that ICT (Information and Communication Technology) has for contributing positively to development in poorly resourced parts of the world.

A comparison of innovation-oriented conventional development and innovation-oriented sustainable development is summarized in Table 10.1. This contains only very generalized ideas and its content needs to be detailed through considerably more discussion.

We need to look further at the characteristics of this new type of innovation, which could well help alleviate some of the many problems associated with uneven development across the world.

Table 10.1 Summarized characterization of two types of innovation

	Innovation for conventional development	*Innovation for sustainable development*
Natural resource	treated as unlimited	treated as limited
Business resources/assets	mostly tangible	mostly intangible
Production/consumption	single mass market	many niche markets
Business field	manufacturing-oriented	service-oriented
Motivation/mission	profit	sense of social responsibility
Investment	large for a few businesses	small for many businesses
Expected growth	J-curve increase	stable, sustainable
Organizational structure	centralized, autocratic	decentralized; unit autonomy
Human relations	vertical, "military"	horizontal, democratic
Business architecture	value-chain, vertical	value-net, networking

We know, of course, that it will not be possible to make all businesses sustainable. Some modernization in the form of mass production and rapid growth may be necessary, particularly for emerging countries. However, from a global perspective, we need to harmonize the sustainable type of business management with the conventional type. The two kinds of management practice should complement each other. We are now responsible for balancing these different business approaches.

Final acknowledgments

The author would like to express his sincere appreciation to his supervisors and colleagues at Kochi University of Technology and the graduate school, particularly Professor Taketo Sakuma (President of the university), Professor Hajime Okamoto (Chief Director of the university), Professor Osamu Tomisawa (ex-Dean of the Management Department).

The author would also like to thank his editors at Routledge, Robert Langham and Lam Yong Ling, for their valuable support.

Bibliography

Anzoff, H. I. (1965) *Corporate Strategy*, New York: McGraw-Hill.

Badaracco, J. L. Jr. (1991) *The Knowledge Link*, Cambridge MA: Harvard Business School Press.

Boyle, D. and A. Simms (2009) *The New Economics: A Bigger Picture*, London: Earthscan.

Brown, Lester (2001) *Eco-Economy: Building an Economy for the Earth*, London: W. W. Norton & Co.

Cooke P. and A. Piccaluga (2006) *Regional development in the Knowledge Economy*, Oxon.: Routledge.

Daly, H. E. (1996) *Beyond Growth: The Economics of Sustainable Development,* Boston MA: Beacon Press.

Feng Liu, M. Hirano and P. Liu (2008) "Regional Development Through Autonomy Establishment in China and Japan – A Comparative Viewpoint Based on Cases of Chengdu Five Golden Flowers (FGF) and Tokushima Kamikatsu-chou", *Multimedia Information Academy Association Journal*, 62/11.

Gawer, A. and M. A. Cusumano (2002) *Platform Leadership*, Cambridge MA: Harvard Business School Press.

Gray, J. (1998) *False Dawn: The Delusions of Global Capitalism*, London: Granta Books.

Hamel, G., Y. L. Doz and C. K. Prahalad (1989) "Collaborate with your competitors and win", *Harvard Business Review*, January–February, 133–139.

Hamel, G. (1991) "Competition for competence and inter-partner learning within international strategic alliances", *Strategic Management Journal*, 12, 83–103.

Harris, J. M., T. A. Wise, K. P. Gallagher and N. R. Goodwin (2001) *A Survey of Sustainable Development: Social and Economic Dimension*, Washington DC: Island Press.

Hawken, P., A. Lovins and L. H. Lovins (1999) *Natural Capitalism: Creating the next industrial revolution*, New York: Little, Brown & Co.

Hirano, M. (2008) *Regional value-creating enterprises: Management strategy in knowledge-based society*, Tokyo: Maruzen Publishing Company.

Horlings, I. (2010) *Vital Coalitions, Vital Regions*, Marijkewig, The Netherlands: Wageningen Academic Publishers.

Human Social Science Department, Kochi University (2000) *2000 Research Report on Kochi, No. 1*, Kochi University, Japan.

Human Social Science Department, Kochi University (2001) *2001 Research Report on Kochi, No. 2*, Kochi University, Japan.

Human Social Science Department, Kochi University (2002) *2002 Research Report on Kochi, No. 3*, Kochi University, Japan.

Inkpen A. C. (2000) “A note on the dynamics of learning alliances: Competition, cooperation, and relative scope”, *Strategic Management Journal*, 21, 775–779.

Inkpen, A. C. (1993) “Learning and knowledge Acquisition through International Strategic Alliances”, *The Academy of Management Executive*, 12/4, 69–80.

Inkpen, A. C. and K. Ramaswamy (2006) *Global Strategy*, Oxford: Oxford University Press.

Ishiguro Y., M. Fujita, N. Maeda, K. Kanai and A. Yamasaki (2003) *Industrial Clustering Strategy in Japan*, Tokyo: Yuhikaku Publishing Company.

Kamakura, T. (2002) *Sango Shuseki no Chiki Keizai Ron* (Regional Economics and Industrial Agglomeration),Tokyo: Keisou Shobou.

Kitagawa, F. (2005) *Art of Hope, Dream of Co-working*, Tokyo: Kadokawa Shoten.

Klein, N. (2007) *The Shock Doctrine: The Rise of Disaster Capitalism*, New York: Picador.

Korten, David C. (1998) *The Post-Corporate World: Life After Capitalism*, West Hartford CT: Kumarian Press.

Krugman, P. (1991) *Geography and Trade*, Cambridge MA: The MIT Press.

Latouche, S. (transl. D. Macey) (2009) *Farewell To Growth,* Cambridge, UK: Polity Press.

Lummis, C. D. (2004) *Can't We Become Rich without Economic Growth*? Tokyo: Heibonsha Library.

Marshall, A. (1890) *Principles of Economics*, London: Macmillan & Co Ltd.

Matsui, K. and S. Yamagami (2006) *The One Product One Village Movement and Developing Countries*, Japan: Asia Economics Laboratory Press.

McDonough, W. and M. Braungart (2002) *Cradle to Cradle: remaking the way we make things*, New York: Farrar Straus & Giroux.

Meadows, D. H., D. L. Meadows and J. Randers (1992) *Beyond The Limits*, White River Junction VA: Chelsea Green Publishing Company.

Meadows, D. H., D. L. Meadows, J. Randers and W. W. Behrens (1972) *The Limits to Growth; A report for the Club of Rome's Project on the Predicament of Mankind*, New York: Universe Books.

Mill, John Stuart (1848) *The Principles of Political Economy*, New York: Penguin Books.

Mishina, K. (2004) *The Logic of Incomplete Strategy*, Tokyo: Toyo Keizai Inc.

Nonaka, I. and H. Takeuchi (1995) *The Knowledge-Creating Company: How Japanese Companies Create the Dynamics of Innovation*, Oxford: Oxford University Press.

Pedersen, P. D. (2009) *The Fifth Competitive Axis*, Osaka: Asahi Shimbun Publishing Co.

Porter, M. E. (1979) *On Competition*, Boston MA: A Harvard Business Review Book.

Porter, M. E. (1980) *Competitive Strategy: Techniques for Analyzing Industries and Competititors*, New York: The Free Press.

Porter, M. E. (1990) *The Competitive Advantage of Nations*, London: The Free Press.

Porter, M. E. (1998) *Competitive Advantage: Creating and Sustaining Superior Performance*, New York: The Free Press

Savitz, A. and W. Weber (2006) *The Triple Bottom Line*, San Francisco CA: Jossey-Bass.

Saxenian, A. (1994) *Regional Advantage: Culture and Competition in Silicon Valley and Route 128*, Boston MA: Harvard University Press.

Schumacher, E. F. (1973) *Small is Beautiful: A Study of Economics as if People Mattered,* London: Frederick Muller Ltd.

Senge, P., B. Smith, N. Kruschwitz, J. Laur and L. Schley (2008) *The Necessary Revolution,* London: The Marsh Agency Ltd.

Index